The Joyful Brand

Personal Branding for Authors, Speakers and the Rest of Us

The Joyful Brand

Personal Branding for Authors, Speakers and the Rest of Us

by Drew Becker

ISBN-10: 1-944662-27-8

ISBN-13:978-1-944662-27-1

Realization Press Publication Date September 1, 2018

Cover Art by Diana Henderson
Cover Design by MAAS Graphics

Dedication

This book is dedicated to numerous people who have bravely taken off their masks and acted from their authentic selves. This began with my family and not surprisingly included my friends. All these role models were daring enough to swim upstream against social currents.

A special recognition goes to Genece Hamby who introduced me to the concept of Personal Branding. Genece leveraged her brand to go on to pursue her artistic career first in the digital medium and then in shoe design. She currently designs patterns for furniture, clothing and other products. Her commitment to design—whether with the original Your Essential DNA Personal Branding curriculum, graphics for websites or in her artistic endeavors—has kept her true to her personal brand, although those who do not know her might not see the connection.

I also dedicate this book to Kristen Joy Laidig and Natalie Marie Collins for their coaching and support through the last six months of the writing. I joined them and other writers online every Friday morning for the Book Writing Challenge and spent the hour scribing or researching in the virtual group. My gratitude is extended to the other writers who also offered their support. This accountability pushed me to get the first draft written in a timely fashion.

Before we begin:

Here is some critical information:

Your Personal Brand portrays

- How You are Distinct

- How You are Notable

- How you articulate your Authenticity

You can discover your brand by considering these questions:

- Who am I?

- What am I meant to do?

- Who am I meant to serve?

A Bit about Me

I am a communicator. This has remained true throughout my career. I began writing before I was ten and probably raised my hand too many times in classes throughout the years, seeking to understand the world around me. I was admonished for speaking out of turn in fourth grade and shamed into not interrupting the class. I thought I wanted to be a psychiatrist or a doctor as I grew up in order to help others through explaining and questioning them.

I graduated from the University of Colorado with an English degree and a teaching certificate and immediately began teaching high school English, but I left after a few years of butting heads with administrators because I believed that learning how to learn was as important, if not more so, than the subject matter itself. I wanted students to solve problems, not just repeat the lessons of the past. I quickly realized the school system was too restrictive for me and I looked for another path.

I worked in restaurants, drove a cab, did some adult training and did other odd jobs. All the time I was writing something, and that writing kept me going even if washing dishes or busing tables didn't fulfill my dreams. I published my first book in 1976 and then returned to contracting and working in companies as a writer or doing customer and sales support.

When I was laid off from my position in 2001, I started a marketing company with a colleague and we were moderately successful. We did traditional marketing—copy writing, press releases and website copy— as well as business development for our clients.

I had a chance meeting with branding expert Genece Hamby in 2005. She had developed the original program to train people to discover their personal brands. I was in the beta program and soon became one of the people who facilitated the program and later was certified as a trainer for others who wanted to facilitate.

Working with her to become a personal branding architect, I edited and discussed concepts and reworked some of her material. The final result became my own program, *Purpose Powered Process (P3)* based on her earlier work.

I wanted to share my knowledge gleaned from guiding a large number of people through the process of personal branding, so I wrote this book. As you progress through the exercises, I hope you uncover your brand, recover some joy and live your life more fully by design rather than by default.

Table of Contents

PART I GROUNDWORK FOR YOUR PERSONAL BRAND: PASSION AND PURPOSE

PART II YOUR PERSONAL BRAND

PART III ACTIVATE YOUR AUTHENTICITY

PART IV ARTICULATE YOUR PERSONAL BRAND

APPENDICES

Foreword

Branding. It's a word that sounds so simple; yet it's incredibly complex. When I changed my original brand to *The Book Ninja* back in early 2015, at first my colleagues laughed at me. They came to me and said, "What silliness are you up to now? Do you really think anyone is going to take that brand serious?" What they didn't know was that I had fallen in love with martial arts and realized I really *was* a ninja when it came to publishing. So not only was I well on my way to earning my black belt (which I achieved in early 2018), but I was taking the martial arts code to the very core of who I was—personally *and* professionally.

Fast-forward to today and that brand has attracted tens of thousands of new students worldwide, won several awards, and even been mentioned on a sitcom! All it took was for me to analyze my*self*. Who am I? What do I stand for? What brings me *joy*?

When I first asked these questions, the book you're holding in your hands right now wasn't yet available to me. But I knew enough about branding to realize it needed to start with *me*. As Drew says in chapter 4, "What Am I Meant to Do?... This concept deals with alignment to your integrated passion-purpose."

Unless you can identify your passions (both past and present) and link them to your purpose (why you are here), you'll be flying blind and scattered all over the place... and your customers will notice! The more scattered you are, the less you will sell. Once you identify your passion, link it with your purpose, and make it what you're *meant to do*, you will notice more customers lined up ready to buy. You've made your*self* and your purpose clear to them. Unless you identify this all-important foundation to your personal brand, your buyers will remain confused about who you are and what you do. And confused buyers don't buy!

Lucky for you, you are holding the roadmap to answer this all-important question… and a whole lot more.

The best part of personal branding is Drew's explanation of how to keep your personal brand intact even if how you present yourself to an audience changes. While a shift in company branding can and often does lose customers, your personal brand is different. It is directly tied to who you are—every layer. As Drew states in chapter 8, "A strong brand does not change even if the presentation does. Your brand should include more than one aspect of yourself so that you are able to tailor the part of it you decide to present." This one tip alone along with the accompanying exercises will help you craft a presentation of your*self* that you can use no matter *what* you choose to do.

For example, in 2018 I launched a new "brand," *The Startup Ninja*. In my own personal growth of starting multiple retail stores in our downtown of Chambersburg, Pennsylvania, I learned my passion is less about books and more about the start-up process. And having earned my black belt by this time in both martial arts and business, I translated the core passion of who I am into the new brand. It's still me; it's still my personal brand. It's just adapted to include *more* of what I'm *meant to do*.

When Drew asked me to write the foreword for this book, I was deeply moved. As a teacher, I admire everything he's accomplished since we started working together years ago. As a colleague, I've learned from him, brainstormed with him, shared meals with him, and can tell you he is the real deal. When I read *The Joyful Brand*, I realized what a goldmine this book truly is. What you're holding in your hands is a roadmap full of exercises and resources to blend your passionate purpose with your life's work—your legacy.

So if you're flipping through this book trying to decide if you should buy it, save your decision-making energy and just add it to your education arsenal. If you've already bought it, congratulations! You've just made one of the best decisions you'll ever make. Take the time to go through all the exercises. Craft your brand. Live your purpose. And by embracing every layer of *you* and what you're *meant to do*, you *will* change your world!

Kristen Joy Laidig
The Startup Ninja™
Author of *Asskickonomics: The Powerful Unseen Force Behind Every Entrepreneur*

Opening Remarks

When I first began working with the concepts in *The Joyful Brand: Personal Branding for Authors, Speakers and the Rest of Us*, I intended the book to help solo entrepreneurs who were starting new companies. One of the failure points for new enterprises was not, as I expected, underfunding but was instead the inability to persist when needed. I saw people, including myself, put time and energy into their businesses only to bail out before the endeavors were profitable, because they lost motivation and commitment.

I believed many of these entrepreneurs were nearly there, but they could not see that. Having started and stopped on multiple projects to build my own businesses, I understood. After all, many mornings I woke up not quite ready to take on what the day would hold. After completing the personal branding program and training others in the process, I experienced firsthand the commitment it created and saw it help those who were tempted to quit to find the inner motivation to continue.

When I committed to writing the book, I was still thinking about entrepreneurs, but, while working on the manuscript, I began mentoring and publishing writers and speakers and realized that personal branding would be extremely useful to them as well. Like solo entrepreneurs, writers and speakers need to persuade audiences that their products—books and speeches—are valuable and worthy of the investment.

I also had the opportunity to present this material through a community college to job seekers. Many thanked me for the short course which helped them clarify what kind of employment they pursued. Some of the participants confided that this experience was one of the factors that helped them change perspectives and become better candidates for their desired employment. Finally, I recalled presenting some of the concepts to teens who were contemplating what to do with the rest of their lives.

I included examples for writers and speakers as well as for others who could benefit from going through the personal branding experience. I have included some of my stories about challenges I faced developing my personal brand. I changed the title to *The Joyful Brand: Personal Branding for Authors, Speakers and the Rest of Us* to reflect this wider focus.

I have included exercises throughout the book. Although they may be done independently, they are arranged in a progressive order to create your brand. You will see that the numbering is sequential throughout the book to encourage completing each of them in order since they build on each other.

This book is for anyone who wants to improve their quality of life through self-discovery because personal branding fosters a deeper understanding of yourself. The results of the exercises can provide marketing materials, but the knowledge about your purpose and passion provides so much more: a sense of confidence and drive to live a richer life.

How to Use This Book

This book is not a short guide to personal branding but rather a detailed discovery of the process and concepts behind building your own personal brand. Some readers might want to use the book to work through the exercises without the additional descriptions of the concepts behind these exercises. For those readers, I suggest you read the first chapter and then the chapters that include the exercises in chapters 2-3, 8 and 11-15. For those who want a fuller understanding, it will be helpful to read all the chapters, and, for those who want even more details about the history of the process and the concepts of perception, language and impact, also read the appendices.

For serious readers who want to study personal branding and build their own brand, read the entire book front to back.

The appendices contain additional information:

- Appendix 1 is a brief history of the programs on which the book is based.

- Appendices II-IV are detailed descriptions of perception, language and impact, each briefly described in chapter 7. These are separate because they are more technical and may not be of interest to people who are not writers or speakers or do not wish to discover this additional material.

- Appendix V and VI have other supplemental information. Appendix V deals with challenges to your personal brand. Appendix VI is included to be transparent. Of the many participants we have taken through the process, a few did not complete the course for various reasons. This appendix tells about those participants.

- Appendix VII contains footnotes and a list of the worksheet used throughout the book.

Introduction

Throughout this book I will talk about personal branding for authors and speakers as well as for others because a personal brand can help anyone. I will address the authors and speakers in Chapter 4 and continue with that material throughout the rest of the book. First, I will cover the fundamental concepts that apply to everyone.

JOY

What is joy?

Joy is one of the deepest feelings you can experience as a human being. Is it a sense of well-being or is it more than that? Is it enjoying what you desired and attained or is it more than that? Is it the result of being lucky or is it something more? Is it gratitude for what you have? Is it a chuckle or snort after hearing, "Ya need an ark? I Noah guy."

Joy touches the core of who and what you are. This feeling lifts you and those around you because it is as contagious as a smile. It reaches your depths because it is your fullest expression, and that is why your personal brand can bring joy it represents this self-knowledge.

Note: This book includes exercises for you the reader to complete to build your brand. As these exercises are introduced beginning in chapter 2, the results from an undisclosed participant will be presented. "Gwen" is an author and speaker as well as having her own business. I hope that her responses will be useful in guiding you. Additional examples from other participants are also included.

WHAT DOES YOUR PERSONAL BRAND DO FOR YOU?

What's the big deal about personal branding? Nobody even knew what it was a couple of decades ago, so why is it important today for authors, speakers and the rest of us? And while I'm introducing the idea, why is it *joyful*? Great satisfaction comes when you can easily express to others what you do in a way that entices them. When you have your personal brand, you can engage prospects and clients with the turn of the right phrase that resonates from deep in your core and emanates your powerful purpose and passion. This expression brings joy and makes you memorable.

Your personal brand can be magnetic and attract others who will want to work with you. Have you ever noticed at a networking event that those who seem to draw others to them exude a sense of excitement and bring strangers into conversation easily? They have a clear message that speaks to and attracts people. These folks have discovered their personal brand and know how to express it.

At the same networking event, those without an excellent personal brand lack the ability to generate excitement and power to keep others engaged. They are not as capable of communicating with fellow attendees and don't pull others to them. Without a clear understanding of their purpose and passions, they find it difficult to engage people and don't generate much interest. They are quick to try to sell rather than build a relationship based on commonality. Without understanding their personal brand, they cannot energize those around them.

Having a personal brand can help you differentiate yourself when you meet people. Very few of us do not have competitors. Why would someone want to work with you instead of someone else in the same field? The answer is tied to your personal brand since people buy/work with people they know, like and trust. Your personal brand can fuel all three of these factors.

I have been working with clients to build personal brands since 2002. Since then I have partnered with others to develop a program and taken 100-plus individuals through one of many variations of this remarkable process. I have worked with entrepreneurs, students, authors, speakers and employees to develop their brands. I decided to share this with more people by writing this book. In the Appendix you can read about the evolution of the program, and you will learn how some of the participants have completed the process with the examples I have included in the book. You will also be invited to engage in these exercises as you read so you too can build your personal brand.

BRANDS AND PERSONAL BRANDS

BRANDING

The word branding dates back to the 1550s. It meant "a mark made by a hot iron especially on a cask, etc., to identify the maker or quality of its contents." It has since been used to denote a mark made by a branding iron that is heated and used to identify livestock. However, in the 20th century, its meaning extended into the world of marketing to refer to the image and other attributes of a product.

Drew Becker

We live in a branded world. Big companies invest huge resources to create recognizable brands and we react to them. People tend to buy a brand they are familiar with and support those companies that project a strong brand. The following quote is from a 2013 study:

> *Sixty percent of global consumers with internet access prefer to buy new products from a familiar brand rather than switch to a new brand, according to a new study from Nielsen.[1]*

Branding is so prevalent that you rarely acknowledge it consciously, even though you are bombarded by corporate branding every day. When you see the outline of Mickey Mouse ears or a certain castle and fairy, you instantly know it's Disney. All you have to do is notice a swoosh design on tennis shoes to recognize Nike. These have become so familiar that you don't think about identifying them; you simply assimilate the awareness of the brand. Because of the distinct style of illustration and expression, you could hear a Dr. Seuss story without having read that particular one and likely recognize the author, and all you have to see is a certain red-and-white stovepipe topper to evoke the memory of the clever book *The Cat in the Hat* and a lot of others written by the author. Baseball, football, basketball and other professional and college sports teams have brands represented by their names and logos. We all know the Cubs, the Cowboys, the Warriors. In fact, the controversy about the Redskins may be more about changing branding than about political correctness. People become loyal to brands and feel comfortable with them. Many people resist when product packaging changes, and expensive ad campaigns often follow altered logos, product packaging or other aspects of brands.

So what does this illusive term *brand* mean? There are multiple definitions, but most have this in common: A brand is an overarching idea portrayed in images (logos and common graphics), written copy (product descriptions, websites, press releases, and other text-based communications) and social media (including Facebook, Instagram, Snapchat, Twitter, Google Plus and other platforms, blogs, videos and whatever new web-based fad emerges next). The brand creates loyalty by offering consistency and recognizability as well as promoting trust based on prior or expected experiences with these products or services. Once the trust factor is strong, the brand is a powerful way to keep customers and clients returning for more instead of looking for somewhere else. In our busy world, we rely upon brands so we can automatically and quickly shop and purchase products we already know. The same is true of services.

One example that is evident applies to cars. When I grew up, one of my neighbors worked for Chevrolet as a salesman, and, long before I could own a car, I had a favorite. When my father sold his '55 Chevy, I cried. Even though it would be a few years before I could drive, I expected to get that car. Even though my first car was not a Chevy, I bought a number of them over the years until I found another favorite car brand. I stayed with that brand for over a decade and only changed again when they did not offer features I wanted. To this day I still have an affinity for Chevy and would pick it in an instant over its other American competitors.

PERSONAL BRANDING

In the same way that corporations have long understood the importance of branding, individuals came to realize its importance in the early 1990s. Rock stars and other entertainers were some of the first to intentionally brand themselves. The Beatles brand first featured their mop-top hairstyles and other physical factors that became immediately recognizable. Later we knew them from their *Sgt. Pepper's Lonely Hearts Club Band* outfits. Fat red lips with a tongue hanging out represented the Rolling Stones. Liberace was known for his glittery wardrobe and candelabra.

Oprah had one of the first international intentionally-created brands, which is still going strong decades later. Her brand, which began as a TV talk show hostess, expanded to author, actress, clothing provider, production company, television and radio network owner, online shopping site provider for beauty and food products and more.

Oprah's brand expansion is a great example to begin to understand what a personal brand actually is. A brand, along with the previous definition above, is *a promise* to customers, clients, consumers and other followers. Everything that is attached to the brand carries out the same promise. When you think of a commercial brand like Disney, there is an implied guarantee for wholesome family fun. LeBron James is called *The King*. His brand reflects his superior basketball skills, and he is branded as the best player since the beginning of the 21st century. Whether he wins or loses, he is seen as the central focus of the team wherever he plays. For some, his title means he is the best player ever. Regardless of who is the best player, the brand remains intact.

Another example is Richard Branson's brand with his Virgin Group, which is an umbrella for over 400 companies. He started with a record store and then expanded to a record label and recording studio. Branson grew more by adding Virgin Atlantic Airlines and has gone on to take on the big challenges of our world from climate to going into outer space. His brand is that of the risk-taker and the rebel who found his own path to do what he thinks is important.

Someone with a similar brand but unique unto himself is Elon Musk, CEO of Tesla and SpaceX. He has taken Tesla from being simply a car brand to a technology brand. Formerly Tesla Motors and now Tesla, Inc., the company has reached into the field of diversified energy products. Musk himself and by extension his companies are known for pushing the envelope, innovating and looking to the future. This brand exemplifies the visionary and promises to keep expanding its mission to better the planet and, like Branson, also extend into space.

WHAT MAKES UP A PERSONAL BRAND?

Personal branding has many components. From an authenticity perspective, yours must begin with you—whether you are an author, speaker, a business owner or someone with a different calling. So where do you start to look at you? Begin at your core. But what lies at the core of every person? The answer is universal and unique.

The universal aspects of your brand include your handle or how people identify with you. Although you are an individual, you have a lot in common with everyone else. Finding these shared characteristics with those who resonate with your brand is part of the process.

The unique aspect at the core of each personal brand is built around passions and purpose as we will explore in detail in this book. Many paths lead to this exploration, and unleashing your creativity also brings you to the horizon to see this part of your core.

By finding the effective mix of your unique and universal elements, you can build the foundation for your brand.

This mix will be reflected within your brand both tangibly and intangibly. These concepts will also be uncovered in the pages of *The Joyful Brand*. So, let's jump in head first and explore your passions.

SUMMARY

Passion and purpose are critical in building your personal brand.

A personal brand can be magnetic and attract others who will want to work with you.

A brand is an overarching idea portrayed in images, written copy and social media that creates loyalty by offering consistency and recognizability

A personal brand begins with *you*—whether you are an author, speaker, a business owner or have a different calling. What lies at the core of every person is universal *and* unique.

PART I

GROUNDWORK FOR YOUR PERSONAL BRAND: PASSION AND PURPOSE

The passion rebuilds the world for the youth. It makes all things alive and significant.

—*Ralph Waldo Emerson*

Without passion man is a mere latent force and possibility, like the flint which awaits the shock of the iron before it can give forth its spark.

—*Henri Frederic Amiel*

The purpose of life is a life of purpose.

—*Robert Byrne*

Without passion and purpose, a personal brand cannot be built. This section addresses buried passions and how they are awakened. Adding purpose creates the other element, and combining these forms the basis for a personal brand. This section focuses on the concepts necessary to understand how to build a personal brand. Be patient as you read through Part I since you will work on the brand in the following sections. The exercises in this part of the book are the building blocks, so, although not referred to as branding per se, they are essential to the complete process.

Chapter 1

Passion Born, Buried and Revived

The frenzied mother cannot coax her son down from his makeshift fort high in the old oak. She can't tear her daughter away from playing veterinarian with the dog. They do not seem to hear her as she calls them to eat lunch. Her delicious meal is getting cold. Her children are lost in their passions. As she corrals them, she inadvertently breaks their spells. They are at home in their imaginations, living outside time and space and resist re-entering to the *real world*.

Webster Dictionary defines passion as "a strong liking or desire for or devotion to some activity, object, or concept; an intense, driving conviction." We all have had such experiences at some time in our lives, usually as a child. Each of us has discovered an activity or hobby that thrills us. These activities take us, like the children, out of time. What I mean by that is we lose track of the hour and other obligations and tasks we may have planned for ourselves.

When we get *caught up* in something we are passionate about, we do not respond to others. We are focused in the presence of our activity and can easily ignore the outside world.

PASSIONS BORN

As a child, you began with an innate sense of passion for some activity or another, whether playing with a certain toy or climbing trees. Your parents may have a hard time interrupting this *obsession* even to persuade you to eat or go to sleep at night.

Passion develops from your natural curiosity and, as you explore, you find and pursue things that fascinate you. Whether flying a kite or reading a book, under the influence of your passion, as a child you resist attempts to change your course of action to please others. If not squelched, these activities you loved as a child could have bloomed into life-long passions.

As an adult, these joy-producing pastimes can be difficult to uncover since you may have forgotten them or may be reluctant to share them with others. In fact, most adults do not think about or talk about passions at all.

There are exceptions. Passion is easiest to recognize in artists like musicians, who are driven to create and perfect the next song, or painters, who produce canvas after canvas. It is also evident in entrepreneurs who thrive on creating businesses and making them successful. Other visible examples are the best athletes who continuously strive to make their game better. However, for the rest, the ideas are forgotten in favor of everyday tasks and obligations as grownups.

You do not have to be recognized or rewarded to be passionate about an activity. Many people who pursue their passions make the interest into a hobby rather than a profession. I've known programmers who have great passion for playing music although they would never consider trying to be professional musicians. One person, Chris, has a passion so strong he would rather stay home for days and play guitar but realizes he has to make a living. Pursuing his passion keeps him motivated and enhances his enjoyment of his daily work as a software architect.

Do you have only one passion? More often than not, no. Most of us have multiple passions that can scatter our focus; different stimuli trigger interests in distinctive passions. The well-documented "shiny object syndrome" in some cases may be a result of being driven by several passions. This entanglement of desires can create some challenging situations.

What is a more severe problem, however, is that many of us as adults do not follow passions because we have buried or forgotten them.

WHAT HAPPENS TO PASSION?

I meet people every day who think they are in touch with their passions. When I ask what they are passionate about, they either cannot name it or say something vague or relates to someone else. Here's an example of that: "I am passionate about my husband (or wife or kids)." They don't understand that their passion has to be about themselves!

Some of the signs you have lost your passion are that you daydream about doing something else other than your current occupation or you say to yourself, "If only I had…"

What about those of you who can't identify one or more passions? What happened to that spark that was kindled in childhood? If we are all born with passion (although it may not have bloomed), what happened to so many people who seem to have lost it? It has been buried for assorted reasons.

Many people find it easier to ignore passions than to pursue them. Multiple factors can conspire against following a loved activity.

Buried Passion

How do you know if you have lost your passion? A life coach I know told me that many of her clients do not know whether they have lost their passion or not. If your passion has waned, you might identify with one or more of the following statements:

- I have a sinking feeling, a feeling of dread on Sunday nights when thinking about going to work on Monday.

- I daydream about my perfect life only to tell myself that it is "not possible" or "if only."

- I have forgotten how to dream.

- I have settled for doing something that is convenient and secure out of fear.

Think back and consider what may have caused you to abandon your passions. It may be a single incident, or it may be a combination of events and experiences.

One primary reason you may not be able to ignite your excitement is because it has been buried too long. As you grow up, a sense of duty and practical matters obscure your ability and desire to follow your dreams. Many have given up on activities like playing an instrument, writing a book or designing clothing. These activities have been demoted to *hobbies* which are relegated to take place, if at all, after you have accomplished the daily tasks of making a living, raising a family or both. Since passions are not viewed as a necessity, they can be forgotten, and the daily grind becomes the norm. Working 40-60 hours a week and/or taking care of a family is exhausting, so at the end of the day, you don't seem to have time to pursue a passion.

Do you remember a passion you decided to follow and how someone dissuaded you from the idea? Although I have often heard parents tell their children that they can be anything they want, those same parents are less supportive if the direction doesn't match their vision for the child. Even when told that the sky is the limit in terms of what they can do, children tend to close down if parents determine their direction is unrealistic or not in line with family values and expectations. Did this happen to you?

Now don't get me wrong, I don't think that anyone can do anything; that is not true. We all have limits; however, what are your actual abilities? If you are not endowed with certain physical characteristics, you might not be able to excel in some athletic arenas. If you refuse to learn to swim, you will not be a swimming champion; if you don't read, you will probably not become a great writer.

Some think a child's abilities can be measured, but I am not so sure. What about the small professional basketball players like Muggsy Bogues, Spud Webb, Isaiah Thomas and his son Isaiah Thomas Jr.? I am sure some people thought that they were too short to play basketball and told them so throughout their lives until these remarkable athletes surprised everyone with successful careers. It is hard to predict what can be accomplished, and no one has the foresight to know who the next star might be.

When I was teaching (10 years in the public schools as a full-time English teacher and then as a go-anywhere-teach-anything substitute), I spent a week in a classroom of "low IQ" students. Their lessons were elementary, and they did not hide their boredom, but, when I introduced a current news topic, many jumped at the opportunity to participate and smiles came to their faces. As a former teacher, I know how easy it is to underestimate a child based on test scores, previous accomplishments or apparent efforts.

In addition, how can we make these judgments when we may not even know which skills will be necessary in the future. With the world changing so quickly and consistently, who knows what the next necessary skill set will be. In 1999 in his book, *The Brand You50: Reinventing Work*, Tom Peters predicted "...that 90+ percent of White Collar Jobs will disappear or be reconfigured beyond recognition."[2] He posited it would happen in the next 15 years. It's obvious that the world has changed significantly since then, and new opportunities have come into being while other white-collar jobs have disappeared. How many typewriter repairmen (or women) do you know? The future promises more of the same, so we can only guess what work options will exist in the future. You can only hope that skills learned today can be used, modified or leveraged in novel ways to fit what will be needed. No career path is as certain as it was 50 or even five years ago.

In our society we give lip service to following one's dreams *until* you finish your education and training. It is fine for you as a student to have dreams, but, once you join the working world, you will have little societal support. How many times have you heard people in a corporate environment encourage someone to strike out on his or her own? Not very often. The message you hear repeatedly is to hold onto that job and take care of financial obligations, keep your health insurance and other benefits, and be grateful for a steady paycheck. This is in part corporate or company culture. These messages about security are also a projection from others who are fearful about taking such risks. Companies do not benefit if their workers exit and do not continue to add to their profits. It is doubtful that you will get much encouragement to follow passions inside most workplaces.

Another factor is that many adults are content to go to work, do their jobs, get paid and start their *real lives* when they walk out of the workplace. For some the nine-to-five grind is so exhausting that it leaves many too tired to think They want to get home and just relax. A young lady recently told me she does not read or consider poetry because it makes her think. Once she has left work, she wants to dedicate her life to play.

Many abandon their passions because those ideas are put down by family, peers and/or friends. Many family members will deride you if you stray from a safe and secure path. Most parents want their children to take care of themselves and gain financial security before venturing out to riskier pursuits.

Unfortunately, aspiring authors and speakers hear this type of response all too often. Many are subject to this type of misunderstanding and negative comments, and people who may be gifted never venture out to discover if they do have the ability and persistence because someone else has discouraged them.

One of the more recent poignant events occurred as I was eating lunch in a fast food restaurant. A mother with her three children came in, ordered and then marched over to a table. There the four of them planted themselves to wait for their order. The mother pulled out her cell phone and buried herself in what was probably Facebook. The four-year old, the nine-year old and the 13-year old followed suit (yes, they all had smart phones!), and, after the 13-year old brought the meals back to the table, they each returned to their phones. When the nine-year old asked a question, the mother looked up perturbed to be interrupted from reading a post on social media. This was the first time she raised her head from the phone since sitting at the table.

This lack of recognition of her own child demonstrates a modern cycle that stunts growth. Smart phones as a cultural phenomenon contribute to isolation. Isolation leads to an underdeveloped sense of self-worth. When you have low self-esteem, you don't feel worthy enough to pursue your passions. You may think, "I'm not important, how can my passions be important?" This low self-esteem can kill the discovery of passion in many people.

These are a few of the reasons I believe relate to low self-esteem in our lives:

- Detrimental messages are ingrained in parents and passed down to children.

- Defensiveness and failure to share result from sibling rivalry.

- Jealousy of others who you perceive as better limits you.

- Comparative thinking is a most powerful degrading factor.

Low self-esteem is epidemic in our competitive culture.

DETRIMENTAL MESSAGES

Why do we live in a world of so much negativity? When writing a blog recently, I was looking for the average number of times per day children hear the word "no." One source stated that a one-year-old hears it over 400 times a day (146,000 times a year)[3] That can result in devastating a child's ego. Regardless of the exact number of times, we know this happens often.

Listen for one day to hear how many times someone (maybe you) is discouraged by detrimental comments. Listen in the line at the grocery store or while you are waiting for food in a restaurant or as you are talking with friends. I hope you will not hear it from friends, but listen anyway. Finally listen to yourself and see if you catch yourself responding negatively.

DEFENSIVENESS

Why do some people feel they have to defend themselves at every turn? It may be that person was attacked physically, psychologically or in another way by siblings or others when growing up. These defenders learn techniques to protect themselves and may carry them into adulthood whether necessary or not whenever they do not feel in control. Having to be aware of an attack—real or perceived—at all times has critical effects on communication and interaction skills. Passions are not something you can think about when you are more concerned with basic needs like safety. In Abraham Maslow's hierarchy of needs, self-actualization happens only after the psychological, safety, belonging and esteem needs are met. Examples of safety can be extreme where bodily harm is threatened or subtler where constant jabs at the ego wear down the sufferer. One response is to consider oneself a victim and hide from a fruitful life with victim behaviors.

FAILURE TO SHARE

I don't know how I became jealous as a child except that, with three younger sisters, I probably competed for attention and felt deprived when I did not get it. When my parents moved away from their families just before I was born, they left relatives behind. Several of their new friends became my surrogate aunts and uncles. I remember an incident when I was eight or nine years old and the oldest of my sisters and I were with Aunt Norma, a school psychologist, and I was playing solitaire with a deck of cards.

When my sister asked if she could play, I responded, "No, I am playing with these cards; you can't have them."

Aunt Norma replied, "Why are you acting like that with your sister?

Do you think there is just one deck of cards? You might want to think about what you just did." I felt my face go red as she brought out another deck.

This must have made an impression since I remember it to this day. I felt the need to guard what was mine so badly that I never considered that my sister could play with that other deck. I am still ashamed today when I think back, but this taught me a lesson and, whenever I found myself being defensive about sharing (jealous that someone else would get my piece of the pie), I recalled this and looked to see if there was another way to interpret the situation.

JEALOUSY

Jealousy is another reason we guard ourselves. We ask ourselves, "What does he or she have that I do not; how is that person more capable than I am?" It is convenient to use this excuse for not performing or not completing a project.

Jealousy like failure to share is another reaction to competing for attention. This competition makes some children withdrawn, others aggressive, and still others passive-aggressive. Does this influence your life, the lives of your siblings, and/or of your children? Think about this to determine how it might have stifled you and may still be an impediment. Listen again for responses from others that indicate jealousy as you go about your day.

COMPARATIVE THINKING

Comparative thinking is another impediment that can hinder growth in children and adults. You tend to see yourself in relation to others. This begins in childhood with siblings or with other children. You look around and see what you have and compare it to what others have, and you hear comparisons of others to yourself more often than you are aware.

Television, mass media, and more recently social media dictates what is fashionable and how you think you should look. There is an inherent urge to compare yourself to those you watch on media, and advertisers take advantage of that by selling products that they tell you overtly or subtly will make you like these celebrities. You consume a ton of information about body image, the best and most stylish shoes, what you should eat and drink and how you should act daily. This influences you in your perceptions of yourself and others.

How often does a parent inadvertently say, "Randy, why can't you act nicely like your sister/brother does?" This type of statement sets up and reinforces comparative reactions in your mind. Fuel is added to the fire, perhaps daily, as you grow up. The fodder for comparative thinking, which comes not only from your family during childhood but also from many other sources in your environment, becomes a powerful force.

Schools use grading to track progress and achievement for students, but the side effect is the student sees grades as a ranking system. Many parents put undue pressure on children to excel and to earn top scores. The reasoning is that, with the competitive nature of getting into the best schools at the next level, whether kindergarten or graduate school, having good grades is paramount to success. This concept is part of the social fabric in America as well as many other countries around the world.

When Randy has a B average while his sister Beth gets all As, there is a tendency for parents and teachers to try to get Randy to match that same level regardless of his abilities. Although our culture has more sensitivity to individual differences than it did 25 or 50 years ago, comparisons still are voiced. We are constantly comparing one person to the next.

Is it human nature to do this? I think not. Instead this is a learned behavior—grandparents to parents, parents to children and on and on. As a former public school teacher, I observed this cycle. When I talked to parents about pressure to get good grades, most traced it back to their own parents or used the phrase, "I want my kids to have the things I didn't have." To attain those things, children have to get good grades.

This pressure forces students into a mold where they try to conform to achieve these educational expectations or they rebel and display symptoms like withdrawal, disruption, bullying/distain, escapism and/ or boredom.

All these factors lead to an epidemic situation in our culture: low self-esteem. Cultivated by these and other trends and leveraged by a consumer-oriented educational system, you and your dreams can easily be squelched.

Low Self Esteem

Low self-esteem comes from a distorted image of yourself. You have a lot to offer, and just because it doesn't coincide with what others think, that does not diminish it. This disease infects everyday lives.

The Conformist

In order to please parents and other authority figures, most youngsters do what is asked of them. In striving to achieve and meet expectations, they follow whatever rules are presented. Many are happy following this course of action, gliding through childhood and into adolescence with ease. However, once they arrive at adolescence, the natural increase of hormones often challenges this strategy, and they may morph into one of the faces of rebellion.

It is probably a natural activity to oppose the norm during adolescence. During this phase of life you begin a self-definition process that often begins by rejecting what has been acceptable to this point.

You want to be different from your parents. I believe this is a healthy response during the teens and twenties. If this reaction is not explored, significant difficulties may arise later in life.

I do, however, know a few people who navigated through life without this rebellion and have been successful and happy. One such person knew what he wanted to do since he was eight years old. He pursued his goal until he achieved it and plans to happily retire in that profession. Much of the rest of his life mirrors the ease with which he followed his vocation. He is the exception to the rule as far as I can tell.

THE REBELS

Adolescence is a turbulent, difficult and challenging time. The expectations others have of you at this age do not match what you are experiencing internally. There is a conflict during the teen years, which is something of a double bind. This double bind occurs when two competing tendencies are working against each other. On the one hand, as a teen, you want to fit in while on the other hand, you want to stand out as you begin to express your own uniqueness. One of the manifestations of this is sporting rebellious styles that both distinguish one generation from another and show the need to express that individuality. It is interesting that adolescents do not recognize the conformity of their rebellion: wearing certain clothes, having special hairstyles, tattoos or body piercings. These style decisions usually upset the older generation, and that is part of their intent. They also help young folks to stand out from other generations (I grew up and had long hair and a moustache). At the same time, however, they create another set of norms for that generation and obscure authenticity. What appears to be individualistic is merely another collection of patterns gladly shared. This identification with the group is also healthy but delays finding what is unique about you. This is the same double bind at work.

The following sections explore some of the ways that rebellion shows itself. You may see overt and aggressive actions or subtle and passive responses in rebellion.

WITHDRAWAL

One of the classic rebellious reactions is to withdraw. Few parents are spared the anguish of trying to communicate with a teenager and being met with silence. This is a frustrating situation for the parent since the teen is old enough to reason but will not be engaged. As a teacher I encountered a few adolescents who remained quiet even when asked to respond. Some refused to be a part of the class. Most of them made it through school without too much trouble because they completed assignments and did not disturb the classroom.

DISRUPTION

The rebel we are most familiar with is the antagonistic person who disrupts the environment around him or her. This may be in a classroom, in the home, or in any social situation. This form of rebellion calls attention to the perpetrator and he or she garners a great deal of attention. You see this behavior in pets as well, especially when they feel neglected and crave attention. Whether animal or human, the negative attention reinforces the behavior and can create a habit that is difficult to break. As long as the subject is receiving the attention, punishments rarely are effective to curb the behavior.

In the classroom, I considered disruptions by students as cries for help. What part of their lives was unfulfilled and prompted this sometimes-constant need for attention? Was he or she seeking recognition or was something more severe the underlying cause? Whatever the case, the resolution was rarely simple. Sometimes a conversation to reveal a different viewpoint of the situation (Your fellow students don't think you are amusing, justified, etc.) brought about resolution if the problem was not severe, but more often the underlying problems could not be resolved quickly.

BULLYING/DISDAIN

Studies have shown that bullying is related to low self-worth projected onto others. Research shows that abuse, prejudice and bullying are learned behaviors. These traits are learned from parents, other siblings, teachers, coaches and others who are in charge. It may also arise from peers. In the case of parents bullying children, the parents may have been victims of previous bullying. Cycles like these are hard to break and perpetuate the bullying behaviors. The bullying crisis has received national attention due to the pervasiveness of the problem today.

ESCAPISM

Another display of rebellion is escapism. With the advent of the virtual world ranging from video games to social media, another method of hiding from passions has surfaced. A portion of the population has retreated into a virtual world. Many cannot go more than a few minutes without checking cell phones, and the majority of their social interaction is via technology. Technological communication itself is not detrimental; it is only when people use it as a substitute for face-to-face conversations that it becomes escape.

Use of drugs and alcohol and addictions to other things from TV to sex are avoidances and obscure the ability to pursue passions. Spending hours and hours in front of a television set is one way to avoid the acknowledgment of what might feed the passion.

BOREDOM

Boredom is a flavor of withdrawal. This rebellious reaction manifests as a lack of interest in some arena of life. Being bored is a great excuse not to do something. How many times does a student say, "I'm not interested in math or history or English, so I'm not going to (1) participate in class, (2) do the homework, or (3) pay attention. I won't need to know this for my job in the future, so forget it!"

Adults also may ignore tasks they don't want to do because they are boring and prefer to suffer the consequences instead of taking responsibility.

Like all other reactive rebellions, the result of this one is to avoid responsibility and action. Each time someone evades a task, it is added to others he or she has not done. This pile of inactions mounts up in the subconscious. This stuff can keep a person from doing what is really important and thus passion can be obscured in yet another way.

ACTIVISM

Activism can be a beneficial form of rebellion. When you decide to get active and do something about a situation instead of turning your back on it, you move toward a goal instead of away from one. This can fuel and even reveal a passion that has been left fallow.

When constructive, this is one of the only forms of rebellion that can help *build* passion; the ones mentioned above detract and divert people from finding and cultivating their deepest desires.

With the detrimental forces of rebellion pressuring them, most people take the path of lesser resistance and give up, finding some work that is more or less fulfilling, and passions sink below awareness. Thinking about a lost passion is painful and often depressing.

All these forms of rebellion address something missing in how we grow up. I believe being cut off from your passions as you enter adolescence leaves you vulnerable to the rebel mentality and can carry it far beyond adolescence. The buried passions must emerge somewhere else in your personality.

Summary

As a child, you begin with an innate sense of passion for some activity or another.

Many people find it easier to ignore passions than to pursue them. Multiple factors can conspire against following a loved activity.

How easy it is to underestimate another person based on test scores, previous accomplishments or apparent efforts.

It is fine for you as a student to have dreams, but, once you join the working world, you will have little societal support.

Many abandon their passion because those ideas are put down.

A few of the reasons related to low self-esteem in our lives:

- Detrimental messages are ingrained in parents and passed down to children.

- Defensiveness and failure to share result from sibling rivalry.

- Jealousy of others whom we perceive as better limits us.

- Comparative thinking is the most powerful degrading factor.

Low self-esteem comes from a distorted image of yourself. Reactions vary and range from conformity, rebellion, disruption, withdrawal, bullying, boredom, escapism and activism.

Chapter 2

Re-awakening Passion

NOTE: As exercises are introduced we will follow Gwen, an author and speaker who also has her own business. I hope that her responses will be useful in guiding you. Additional examples from other participants are also included.

For many, a time comes in life where the rewards for working in an uninspired job are no longer enough or worthwhile. Sometimes this comes with a loss, or it may result from intense discomfort. However, after you re-awaken your passion, you can recover that joy in your life that previously propelled you into a confident and enthusiastic attitude toward work, family and friends. You are actively linked to the world around you and wear a smile that surfaces from within.

We all recognize when someone entering a room is driven by his or her passion. This person is animated and shows a genuine interest in others. When you are passionate about what you do and the life you live, you have a contagious attitude and attract others to you or make that extra effort to engage them. This has been described as making the room light up when you arrive.

Imagine yourself revitalized and passionate again about your life or feeling a deeper commitment. Each encounter with another person is an adventure; each new challenge is an opportunity to hone your skills or learn something new. You see the world new and fresh; the leaves on the trees are a little brighter, the sun on your skin feels a bit more pleasing. You can enjoy any experience—whether a flat tire on the side of the road turned into a time to meditate and count your blessings or led you to making a new friend and finding interests in common and sharing your knowledge—and use it to motivate you to continue your day with energy and vigor.

To arrive at that recovered passion however may take some effort and introspection that brings up incidents that need to be investigated to get past obstructions that are blocking the joyful you from emerging.

Many incidents can trigger this realization or crisis (Consider the Chinese pictographs for crisis which is danger and opportunity):

- Downtime

- High frustration

- Losing a job

- Personal loss

- Health Issues

- Divorce and separation

- Lack of motivation

- An epiphany

- Empty nest

EXPLORING THE TRIGGERS

DOWNTIME

One of the unintended consequences of returning from a vacation is how difficult it can be for you to go back to work if the job is not fulfilling or is tedious. Taking a few days away from the routine can prompt you to review your employment situation. You might return to work and just grumble, but you might have been changed by getting away and begin planning a new phase of your life. With a renewed vision of what your work might be, the seeds of discontent can pollinate the search for new opportunities.

HIGH FRUSTRATION

During your working lives, at one time or another, you may find your job is too discouraging or aggravating. When frustration hits a critical level, you may quit even without the safety net of other employment. During job transition, you have another chance to consider what your passions are and what new prospects you need to discover that you have not previously explored.

LOSING A JOB

No one likes to be fired, and yet this action can open a new chance never encountered while still employed in the daily grind. Changing what you notice usually shifts what is visible to you. While working day to day, you may not think about building a network, and the opportunities you see are all within the company. When let go, the road to finding another job will be uphill if you are only connected to others in that company and you do not have an extended network of people outside. Of course, you have friends outside work who can be a great help, but how large is that group? If your network is small, you will need to expand it.

This is what I learned after losing my job. I worked with a job transition group for about a year. I attended my first meeting and discussed passion and purpose. This struck a chord and within the month I was tasked with leading the group. The primary purpose of the group was to look for leads for each other, but we also lent emotional support through this difficult phase of our lives. We did what we could to keep each other motivated, because it was often difficult to keep searching after being turned down for a position or having an unsuccessful interview. The thing I learned was that those members who had done some soul-searching about what they wanted were better able to take the rejection and move on. Those who were just looking for a replacement for the previous job were more dramatically affected by an unsuccessful job-seeking experience.

One of the things people in job transition often ask themselves is, "What do I really want to do?" Decisions include whether to seek another position like the one they just left, look for one in the same field, find a new vocation or start a business on their own. These questions in turn require examination to see how their passions will influence the next steps in their careers.

PERSONAL LOSS

The loss of a parent or child forces most people to take stock of many areas of their lives. When my father passed and then a few years later my mother died, I realized I could no longer work in the corporate environment and struck out on my own. Although I had considered doing so before, I always had a pat excuse: I don't know how to do the bookkeeping and don't want to learn. This was effective in keeping me in jobs I didn't enjoy until the crises of losing my parents occurred.

I cannot imagine what it would be like to lose a child. With a loss like that, I imagine (from what I have experienced around those who have) a life is turned inside out. Parents expect their children to outlive them. Everything can be up for re-examination. And, in a tragedy like this, once far enough along in the grief process, there is an opportunity to uncover passions from earlier in life.

I know of people who changed their life course after the death of a close friend. Seeing how tenuous life is, can compel you to cherish every day and be sure that no time is wasted. Many re-dedicate themselves to something they had in common with the person who passed.

HEALTH ISSUES

An illness or accident can trigger this re-examination as well. While I was still in elementary school, I had casts on both legs from toes to thighs, which kept me out of school for about six weeks. The teachers sent assignments home, but I was immobile for part of that time and had to entertain myself while being bedridden. My parents would not allow me to *while away* the hours watching TV, so I began writing. I first wrote a silly soap opera. I listened to these on the radio for a couple of weeks for distraction. I am sure both the plot and the writing were amateurish, but I found I was immersed in the writing and the hours sped by. I think the manuscript was about 40 pages by the time I finished. What was important was that I discovered how much I really loved to write. I also read books during those weeks. Something remarkable emerged from what I considered at first to be a terrible experience.

I know someone who changed her life direction and entered the healing arts after her accident. She had a strong affinity for this new direction but didn't consider the career shift until she experienced healing herself. This life-altering event began what became a successful career. If she had never had the accident, she probably would not have found this passion and acted on it.

DIVORCE AND SEPARATION

Divorce or separation is another traumatic event in many people's lives. During my separation and divorce, I was faced with questions about self-worth, my own behaviors in relationships, assertiveness and passiveness, and a myriad of other issues. One topic that surfaced was what I wanted out of life—a precursor to questions about passions. This can be an opportunity for a new start.

LACK OF MOTIVATION

When you experience an extended period of low motivation, you may question what you are doing. Why do you feel so indifferent? Is your current situation so unsatisfying that you cannot bring any energy to it? Have you outgrown something or someone? Have your values or goals shifted? Any of these circumstances can deflate motivation. If this apathy is intense enough, self-examination may ensue.

EPIPHANY

Have you ever had an epiphany? As you probably know, an epiphany is a deep insight into what's happening in some aspect of your life or in a specific area such as relationships or occupation. If you experience this, a change of direction based on a new perspective can alter your life course. In those cases, passions are often examined during the aftermath.

EMPTY NEST

What happens if your last child grows up and leaves the family? You are faced with new unscheduled time you used to dedicate to your offspring. The altered situation calls for changes and both parents may have more personal time. However, if caring for your children for 18+ years has eclipsed doing what you love, what can happen is another type of crisis. You may need to figure out what to do with your newly-acquired free time. You might have to discern how this reconfigures your relationship. Many changes can occur at a time when children are not the primary, day-to-day concern. You might travel. If you are not free to do so, you could find things to occupy you closer to home. The question of passion can emerge during this stage of life as well.

Although the situation may not be as severe as those described previously, some lesser events may require people to re-evaluate their lives. At this point many feel lost, but often something inside automatically surfaces and the passion from an earlier time comes to the forefront. Do you remember that you used to like to garden or paint or work with your hands? Do you remember the joy of decorating a room or taking time to read a book?

REACTIONS

Some cope with these incidents by sidestepping a radical change and pursuing the passion with a hobby. This may satisfy the longing and present an opportunity to bridge the gap from routine to discovery of the passion.

A friend of mine, Frank Timberlake, picked up his camera and began shooting and, using software, enhancing his photos of landscapes. He has a great eye for astounding pictures of local landmarks. He found that others appreciated his talent, and he now shows and sells his art in galleries and on the internet. His artistic nature has found a release, and his passion has surfaced as he pursues this hobby while continuing to run his company. In fact, he has trademarked his form of art as PhoArt®.

Had he not taken the steps to artistically express himself, he might have fallen into one of the detrimental behaviors described in the last chapter; instead he has enriched his life and surprised his family and friends.

For many, however, this is not enough. A break with current lifestyle, job and/or people is necessary to enable the passion's drive to fertilize the dream and keep it growing.

Once you realize a previous passion is buried and yearning to be released, how do you recover it? Some techniques to return to your earlier passions follow.

Although any one (or a combination) of the events above can trigger a reexamination of your life, some will decide to go on without any changes. This third course of action—to ignore these experiences—results in refusal to explore other options and a lost opportunity for a more fulfilling life.

OBSERVATION CAN TRIGGER A SEARCH FOR PASSION

I mentioned in the Dedication that I was introduced to personal branding through the *Your Essential DNA Personal Branding Program*. While participating in that course, I was given a curious assignment. It occurred in the middle of autumn when Genece, the program initiator, encouraged me to stop and examine the world around me. She advised me to take a break from what I was doing (the usual multi-tasking: thinking about this while doing that) and look at what surrounded me.

"Do it several times a day," she commanded.

By taking merely seconds to add this task of observation to my daily routine, I began to notice the nature around me. As I was driving, for instance, I found that instead of preparing what I might present or ask at the next meeting, I took time to be inspired by the changing scenery around me. The trees and their leaves transitioning into colors before falling were stunning; some late summer flowers were even blooming. I hadn't noticed this beauty before. I peered into other car windows and watched drivers show a variety of different expressions on their faces—fascinating enough to imagine what they were thinking.

My world was transformed, and I caught myself smiling, finding joy in these moments of observation. This cultivated and heightened awareness led to a series of poems, composed on a daily basis by taking time every morning to write just after awakening. This set my intention for the day, and I knew that at least one activity during my schedule was creative, that no matter how uninspiring other events during the day were, I had done one imaginative activity. That knowledge anchored me and reminded me I would create again tomorrow.

PASSION RESURFACES

From discontent to recovery, your journey back to passion can be a long or short trip. It depends on a few factors: depth of the repression, strength of the desire to reinvent yourself, motivation and ability to change. You must move beyond dissatisfaction to begin.

One of the ways to bring passion(s) back is to go through a self-discovery practice. It is just such a process I use to build the passion foundation to help anchor personal brands.

I have worked with branding expert Genece Hamby and with my related process to train people to discover their personal brands. Over the course of a few years, a significant number of people have completed the program which is now called *Purpose Powered Process* (P3). I have chronicled a brief history of the evolution of this program in Appendix I.

Progress

Almost everyone who took the workshops benefited greatly. Over 50 percent made changes in their lives or occupations to be more aligned with their passions.

Those who switched professions or jobs reported a more satisfying life after the change. I will be honest that, as with *my* job and career transitions, the undertaking is not always easy. Let me give you a couple of examples from my life.

I had a new job lined up and was ready to start only to find out that the project was canceled; I spent months looking for new employment before another opportunity presented itself. During that time, there were further disappointments where interviews were difficult to get and those I could book lead nowhere. In looking back, I realize none of those jobs was right for me nor did they fuel my passion. At the time I had not done personal branding work and had not considered my passions as something related to my job hunting. I failed to understand that without true passion for these positions, I could not persuade potential employers that I was the right candidate.

I also had forgotten a significant experience I once had on an airplane. One of the only times I was bumped up to first class, I sat next to an executive from Sony. He was friendly and we started a conversation in which I learned he was a Chief Financial Officer (CFO) for one of the divisions in the United States. I would have considered that a stressful and somewhat dull job, but as we talked I found out nothing could be further from the truth.

"So, what is it that you do?" he asked me.

"I do technical writing for a large corporation and write about software for developers and end users."

"How long have you been doing that? Sounds interesting."

"I've been doing it for nearly a decade, and it is pretty routine after a while."

"Why don't you do something else?"

"I have to support my family. I used to teach high school and liked working with students but left because I detested the politics of the situation. I also moved on because I could not make enough money for my family."

"Can I offer you some advice?" he asked. "I don't do work I don't love. I am excited every single day I go into work and look forward to whatever challenges I will face and let me assure you that some of them are substantial. I look forward to going to work and to coming home to my family when I am not traveling, and I rarely have what some people refer to as a bad day at work."

I was impressed by what he said and thought about it as the flight continued. I remember thinking that he might have this kind of experience as an executive, but I was not in management and had to work for a boss to make a living.

I had temporarily "retired" a few years before after leaving teaching to *follow my passion*. I worked odd jobs to write and published a book but found I could not make a living as a poet and returned to searching for a *real job*. As a result, I forgot this conversation for many years until I started my personal branding training.

When I took stewardship of the personal branding program, I watched many participants struggle with the same disbelief that they could pursue their passion and make a living. Until they could envision themselves delighted with their work, no permanent change was possible.

Those who rediscovered their passions found new energy to either continue on their current path or to make changes in their lives. Those who carried on in the same jobs, lifestyle, etc. had modified their attitudes toward the work or discovered new approaches to keep their work fresh. This newly discovered connection to either a passion from earlier in their lives or to a new, exciting interest prepared them to take the next steps necessary to recover the verve in their lives. They recovered their joy.

Again, to be transparent, I want you to know that for me at times and for a number of participants, the road was not direct. Often people had to take bridge jobs—temporary positions to keep paying for food, housing, and other essentials. However, at the same time, they kept searching for that solution that fueled their passions—whether it was a different position, the same position in another company or a more entrepreneurial action such as starting their own businesses. *What was key was that the passion was recognized*, and goals were set that would enable the individual to live that passion as soon as possible.

Identifying passions is critical to achieving one's goals, whether they be a dream job, a better relationship or any other type of opportunity. Without a clear vision of what you want, it is much more difficult to get it. In my books on writing, I ask readers to spend the first week in different visualization exercises, so the idea of the book becomes concrete. The same is true in accessing passions; if you cannot envision yourself pursuing a passion, it is a pipedream and rarely useful.

When participants examined their passions in the workshop or in earlier one-on-one sessions before the material was modified for a group experience, they thought back to childhood where intense interest in different things was natural and never questioned. When compared to current pursuits, there was often some overlap, but some of the activities no longer held the fascination they once did. Additionally, new interests sprouted. People are dynamic, and change is a constant in life.

What I find intriguing is that many of the interests from childhood carried over into adult life. The way you pursue these may change, but the basic passion is still there.

For example, when I was a child, as I revealed earlier, I loved to listen to stories. I even wrote a few but abandoned that when I became a teacher and later a technical writer. The passion for writing was muffled in the corporate environment until I started writing my novel at night. Every evening I would come home and, before I went to bed, I would work on the novel (which, by the way, is still a work in progress). What was important to me was that after doing extremely structured technical writing during the day, I rewarded myself with free-flowing fiction writing at night. If you are not a writer, you may see this as a double dose of punishment, but many writers will understand how *rewarding* this was.

The passion was for the creativity, not necessarily for the act of writing. While financially rewarding, the daily work did not fuel that desire. It might seem it would serve my passion to write, but it did so in such a limited, uncreative way that it left me unfulfilled. To further feed the passion, I added a time in the morning to look out the same window and write a different poem, an activity that genuinely scratched my creative writing itch.

As workshop participants uncovered and rediscovered their passions, there were always gleams in their eyes and smiles that lit up their faces. This recognition about what they really loved was so strong they could not hide it in facial or body expressions. The passion became a driving force propelling them towards their reachable goals.

Success

What unearthing passions did for most participants was to provide a new inspiration to move forward and find joy in pursuing their dreams.

I also saw an increase in effort and activity which led to success in their endeavors. In this book, you will find some exercises similar to the ones we conduct in the workshop to reveal your passions.

THE PASSION EXERCISES

As adults, you often forget to take time specifically for yourself. Reflective thinking about yourself is critical to the process. You must allow yourself to leave the day-to-day concerns behind when doing the exercises.

NOTE: As a bonus you can get a pdf file for all the exercises in this book. Receive yours by emailing the author at ***Drew@Realization.com*** to get the complementary packet of pdf worksheets. As an alternative, you may order the workbook to accompany this book and keep your exercises together in one booklet.

EXERCISE *1:* UNCOVERING YOUNG PASSIONS

Your first assignment when you decide to build your personal brand is to list childhood activities that brought you joy. You can do this on a computer, but I suggest you write out your list by hand with pencil and paper. The physical activity of writing adds to the power of the process. Number the lines on the page from one to 20. Although 20 may seem like a large number for anything, especially a list from childhood, it is a great target and I believe you can manage it.

Close your eyes and take a deep breath or three. ***Allow your mind to rest***. Stop thinking about what you have to do, what you've already accomplished, where you are going tonight, that you have to do laundry and go to the store before dinner.

Pinpoint your focus on yourself; just think about the breaths you are taking. Listen to the sounds around you. What does your environment feel like? Since you live in a visual society, as long as you have something to look at, reflection is not easy since your attention is focused outside. To accomplish this exercise, you need to look within.

Once you have created that safe space within, recall what kinds of things excited you as a child. These might have been hobbies or activities like climbing trees or swinging or even flights of imagination like being able to fly or pretending to be a train engineer.

When the ideas start to flow, open your eyes and begin filling in your exercise sheet. At first only a few of your activities may come to mind. Up until the entries begin to gush out, relax and don't let the pace of discovery frustrate you. Take time to let this happen. Even after a slow start, most participants can list more than the requested number of responses. Allow time. Often the first 5-10 emerge quickly; then the flow slows. Keep going. Challenge yourself to come up with more. We all have multiple activities that made us happy. If you haven't thought about them for a while, it may take a few minutes to reconnect those synapses in your brain.

You might be surprised at what you remember after a few minutes. Memories flood the senses and you may experience emotions about what you discover.

Almost everyone who has gone through this exercise compiles an extensive list of these pursuits and surprises themselves.

This process has a couple of benefits:

- Compiling the list of passions for later exercises and

- Helping to remember what you have forgotten along the way.

Gwen's Answers:

Childhood Joys

1. Reading fiction

2. Daydreaming/imagining other worlds

3. Being in nature

4. Singing and making up songs

5. Drawing

6. Writing poems and making up stories

7. Creating clay animals

8. Playing with my dog and cats and other animals

9. Learning

10. Hugging trees and stones

11. Listening to music

12. Dancing

13. Excelling in school

Exercise 2: Uncovering Adult Passions

Take a break and then list your current endeavors and interests. This list is usually easier to compile and, not surprisingly, shorter. With the added responsibilities of adulthood, you may find less time to pursue your passions. As you mature, you may lose track of many of your dreams. Bringing these ideas back into your awareness will help drive much of what happens from this point forward in the process.

Think of it this way: If you had all the time and money you needed, what would you pursue? You may consider this question unrealistic if you feel trapped in your daily routine. I am not advocating ignoring obligations and hopping a freight train to a distant land; rather I am suggesting that you introspectively re-examine what brings you joy and design a way to bring it into your life if it is not there already. To illustrate, let me relate one participant's story.

> One participant, whom we'll call Laura, lived in Colorado but had to move East to take care of her aging mother. After her mother's passing, she stayed on at IBM but was not engaged the way she wanted to be.

> After the Purpose Powered Process seminar, she rediscovered her passion and realized a way to fulfill it with her co-workers. She found out that what blocked her ability to feel joy was not her particular job but related to not being able to engage and help those around her to appreciate the fullness of their lives. She realized that she could pursue her passion at work and beyond with every person she met. Hers is a remarkable story and is told in a later chapter.

GWEN'S ANSWERS:

Adult Passions

1. Writing stories, poems, novels
2. Drawing computer art
3. Teaching classes about trees, crystals, angels, healing
4. Interacting with family and friends – deep conversations
5. Playing with our parrots and our new dog
6. Singing and toning

7. Listening to music

8. Learning

9. Seeking spiritual truths

10. Public speaking

11. Movies

12. Editing – making a story/book its best

13. Reading good writing!

14. Hugging trees and stones

15. Being in nature

EXERCISE 3: COLLATE YOUR LISTS

Once you have compiled both lists, compare what both have in common. See what activities, interests, dreams and desires appear on both lists. See if two passions are related. You may find that a passion has morphed to another form.

For example, one might listen to music as a youth, admire a virtuoso and later learn to play piano as an adult. These items are related to appreciating music, but learning an instrument took the passive activity of listening to the level of an active pursuit. Each of the items on the list is an outward expression of a love for music, but playing the instrument is an example of migrating from a dream or desire to actively pursuing that interest.

Some items from childhood fade away. With maturity, wanting to be a fireman or a model may no longer be a realistic or desirable goal. These may have been fancies of youth for most of us, but some desires may still be appealing and may still be possible. We cannot all be professional athletes or movie stars, especially if we do not have certain innate abilities or talents, but a related passion may be uncovered.

GWEN'S ANSWERS:

1. Collated List
2. Reading
3. Writing
4. Learning
5. Drawing
6. Playing with animals
7. Listening to music
8. Being in nature
9. Hugging trees and stones
10. Singing

EXERCISE 4: WRITE YOUR BUCKET LIST

How many dreams, however, have you abandoned without attempting to pursue them? These often come back to haunt you. The concept of a *bucket list* is a grand way to review these dreams. I assume you are familiar with the concept of a collection of things you want to do *before you kick the bucket.*

People raved about the *Bucket List* movie with Morgan Freeman and Jack Nicholson. In the film, the characters escape their aging existences to see how many of their unrealized desires they can accomplish. Although these characters are near the end of their lives, the message applies to people of all ages: Follow your dreams—even if only for one day.

What adventures would you like to have? Don't worry whether or not these are realistic; just write them. Try to record 15-50 items. This exercise is similar to the two previous ones in that when you start only three to five immediately come to mind. Stick with the process until you have a more complete list.

What items are on your bucket list that were not on your current passion list? These may be future passions and indicate natural paths for you as an evolving human being. They might also have seemed too unrealistic to include in your current passion list. Those in touch with passions will find new interests and activities.

One of my favorite themes from a Bob Dylan song is that if you are not busy creating something, you are dying. As you continue on your life journey, you will develop new interests as long as you are open to fresh experiences and to different people. These opportunities will expand your horizons and offer excitement through new experiences. Be open and allow past, present and future passions to emerge.

During this release of the buried passion, you may rediscover parts of yourself that you had forgotten or ignored for many years. Many participants have. This realization is *key* in helping to progress towards a new dedication of purpose.

Gwen's Answers:

Bucket List

1. Having a series of bestselling novels
2. Being a successful writer
3. Speaking to like-minded groups interested in my work
4. Traveling to Glastonbury, UK, and to Scotland
5. Being renowned for saving trees
6. Having my novels optioned for fabulous movies
7. Creating a series of popular meditation CDs
8. Going hang gliding and/or up in a hot air balloon
9. Parasailing again
10. Owning a beach house or mountain getaway

SUMMARY

It is evident when someone enters a room who is driven by his or her passion.

Many incidents can trigger the desire to reawaken passion:

- Downtime
- High frustration
- Losing a job
- Personal loss
- Health Issues
- Divorce and separation
- Lack of motivation
- An epiphany
- Empty nest

One of the ways to bring the passion back is to go through a self-discovery process. It is just such a process I use to build the passion foundation to help anchor personal brands.

Chapter 3

Probing for Purpose

Webster defines purpose as "something set up as an object or end to be attained." I like to think of purpose as the reason to be who you are and do what you do in your life.

Popular literature and psychological theory have been focused on purpose as the motivational factor to keep you moving and feeling a sense of accomplishment in your life. Whether you read *A Purpose Driven Life, Man's Search for Meaning*, or Steven Covey's *The Eighth Habit*, the message is similar: Find the purpose that is a calling beyond the personal. We all have personal goals, and these are helpful to keep us motivated. However, to maintain that momentum you need a greater goal.

If you are an entrepreneur, you might begin your business to make money, but that rarely is satisfying enough to sustain you. An external goal (one greater than yourself) will push you when the going gets tough. A few examples of these goals are:

- To achieve the level of freedom necessary to control your schedule, working when and where you want and easily making time for family and friends

- To assure a secure and comfortable situation for family

- To find and/or support non-profits with which you are aligned

- To purchase a new home

- To build a successful company

- To be recognized as an authority based on a book or speaking

- To be admired by peers

This external driver is stronger than a purely personal goal because it provides an outside motivation and others relying on you.

"DOO BE DOO BE DOO" — FRANK SINATRA

The dual nature of purpose: When contemplating purpose, think of it as having an outer and inner component. The outer purpose can be discovered by an examination of external factors in the environment. The inner purpose evolves from the self-discovery process. The first is aligned with utility, the second with passion.

Outer purpose is the *Do* component in "Doo Be Doo Be Doo;" the inner purpose is the *Be*. You spend most of your life in the *Do* realm, acting, achieving and acquiring, and a minimum in the *Be* realm of meditation, gratitude and self-examination. This is a fact of life in our culture as we pursue security, safety and material comfort. You determine how much of each is necessary. Until you achieve these external essentials, it is difficult to focus on your inner life. No wonder there are three *Dos* and two *Bes*.

Since you spend most of your time *doing* rather than *being*, you are more familiar with the outer purpose. We will examine that, but to get our footing let's begin with a values exercise.

VALUES

Values are the concepts you live by and that you promote in the outside world. Values link people together and are the basis of forming groups from families to social movements. Although they seem to be social, they are in essence personal. Many values are taught to you as a child; others you acquire as you mature.

You can discover your values by talking with a close friend who can provide the reflection you need, or, if you would prefer to do this alone, write your results. Doodling is another method to elicit this information.

EXERCISE 5: EXAMINE VALUES

Take this opportunity to describe your values with this exercise.

1. Discuss your values.

One of the ways to determine values is to look at the opposite. What traits in others bother you? Is it close-mindedness, prejudice, not listening, ignoring others, arrogance? Consider the table below:

CHARACTER	OPPOSITE VALUE
Closed Mindedness	Openness
Prejudice	Non-Judgmental
Not Listening	Great Listener
Ignoring Others	Friendly, Interested in Others
Arogance	Acceptance

2. Make a list or a graphic of 10 values.

3. Rank them in order. If this is difficult, use the dual matching method:

    Consider Value 1 and Value 2 and determine which is more important. Then choose between Value 3 to Value 4. Continue this process until you have halved the number of choices and again until you have the most important value. If you find during in this process that you have discovered your most important value, you have finished.

Determine which values are most important to you, and then see what these values have in common. This can help discover your inner purpose.

Examples:

Jim

Jim was struggling to discover his purpose and did not find it easy to sit still and reflect. He worked with our P3 architects and we began by asking questions.

"What would you change if you could *run the world*?"

This question seemed only to confuse him, and he replied, "There are lots of things I would change, but I cannot even begin to explain it. I wouldn't know where to begin."

"What's the most disturbing thing you see that you would like to get rid of in society?"

"Probably discrimination and bullying." After another few minutes, he said, "Inequities, arrogance and people who don't listen. And I almost forgot to mention whiners and complainers."

"All right, you've got a good list started. Let's begin with those. What are the opposites of these things?"

After a long pause, he replied, "I'm not sure what the opposite of bullying is; is it defending? Discrimination is easy; that's acceptance and treating others with respect."

He now scribbled down the characteristics he dislikes and the opposite values:

CHARACTERISTIC	OPPOSITE VALUE
Discrimination	Acceptance and treating others with respect
Bullying	Defending those who cannot defend themselves
Inequity	Treating all others fairly
Arrogance	Humility
People who don't listen	Listen to others intently
Whining	Be proactive
Complaining	Be proactive

"Let's look deeper into these ideas. How might you promote those values?"

"Being proactive with others and being respectful in all my actions," he replied.

He sat quietly—no small feat for him—for almost 10 minutes.

He then had an aha moment and realized he was driven internally by a sense of justice. He had discovered his inner purpose almost by accident.

Had he not seen the pattern, he could have ranked his values with the technique above.

GWEN'S ANSWERS:

1. Spirituality

2. Living creatively

3. Kindness

4. Peace

5. Wisdom

6. Taking responsibility

7. Speaking truth from the heart

8. Honoring everyone and everything

9. Caring for the planet

10. Helping others

INNER PURPOSE

The "*Be*" considerations are personal (like values) and often more private. This can make them more difficult to share. Inner purpose is based on who you are. Articulating this can be difficult. You may discover this inner aspect of yourself through self-reflection. No one can tell you your inner purpose; you must discover it from within. The nature of inner purpose, however, does not mean that you cannot get help to find it, only that you must be willing to explore and have the desire to open this treasure. Many come across their inner purpose in solitude, some through meditation and others through thought or revelation in a dream or altered state. The aha moment of an epiphany is another source of this discovery.

If you are more kinesthetic, methods include exercise or dance, collage creation, pottery, jewelry making or another artistic endeavor. Movement of all kinds can get you out of your brain and into your body. Once there, the mind is distracted from day-to-day tasks. Thoughts can arise from the subconscious and surprise you at random moments. In the pursuit of something physical, a deeper mental state can surface. If you connect through the body and movement, you may have trouble with written exercises to discover your purpose. You should get outside and move around before engaging in the exercise.

If you are a digital learner, reading, writing and journaling, or word associations may provide this respite from the everyday world. While engrossed in the reading or writing process, you lose track of time and allow the subconscious to deliver messages. Writing exercises may help you delve into inner frameworks.

If you are an auditory learner, listening to or playing music can open your subconscious mind. The auditory experience releases the mind from the everyday. While in reverie, you may hear from the internal voice and receive information. These messages can reveal information locked away for some time. Listening to music is a common activity for many from adolescence into their twenties and beyond. Whether listening to recorded or live music, it is easy for you to be carried away by melodies and rhythms.

If you are a visual learner, a stunning view or a detailed examination of what seems ordinary can trigger a response about the inner purpose. With television, videos on our phones, images on social media (Facebook and Instagram and whatever the next platform will be), YouTube, Facebook Live, etc., the world is primarily visual. Most of us spend a significant portion of our time watching something or observing other people and our surroundings. As a visual, you probably make movies in your head and this can reveal your inner purpose.

The *secret* to this exploration for visuals, digitals and auditories is to find the *quiet place within*. If you who relate kinesthetically, discovering a safe haven for expression serves the same function. In a rushed and sometimes frenetic world, you are challenged to create an island of solitude where thoughts and feelings arise rather than being pushed down into the unconscious. You have an internal essence that knows about your inner purpose; you simply have to make time to discover it. Once the mind is quieted, the ground is fertile for this purpose to reveal itself.

In our workshops, we have a few exercises to create the right environment to entice these ideas to come to the surface. Among the techniques we use are music, guided meditation and silent walks or outdoors activities done while seated with eyes closed. When was the last time you sat outside quietly, shut your eyes and took stock of all the sounds around you? Every day you miss a multitude of these impressions, forgetting that birds chirp, that brooks babble, that the wind rustles the leaves, that a small child expresses glee, that benches creak, or our arms and legs sway freely when gliding on a swing.

In your *do* life, you rarely stop to *be*. *Being* activities bring you back to yourself. You reconnect with your body, with the natural world around you and with each other on a deep level. These activities reveal your inner drivers.

When you consider inner purpose, you go inward to search. This cannot be money or fame; this must be something less mundane. This could be to help others, create security for your family, improve life for the less fortunate, feed the hungry or any number of causes that *go beyond you*. This is often something more noble and directed outward rather than towards self-gratification or even self-improvement.

Some believe inner purpose is set by the Divine. Whether this is true or not, that purpose still must be discovered. Prayer is another pathway to this exploration. No matter how you believe the inner purpose is instilled in us, following this pathway leads to peace and joy and often to success.

EXERCISE 6: INNER PURPOSE

One way to arrive at inner purpose is to ask, "What could I do to make the world better?" Pondering this question changes perspective to one outside the self. Isn't it ironic that you discover inner purpose by going *outside* yourself? Find a quiet place and ask yourself this question about improving the world. Take at least 10 minutes to consider it. You may want to have a piece of paper handy to write down ideas, but after writing close your eyes again and return to the solitude.

Kinesthetics might move around with eyes closed and answer the same question.

Auditories could relax and listen to inspiring music to approach the answer.

An artistic or collage activity is a possible path for visuals.

The answer to the inner purpose question grounds you in the world at a deeper level. People, if they reveal it at all, usually only share this with close friends. This inner purpose provides a more secure anchor than what you generally reveal to others.

GWEN'S ANSWER:

My purpose is to creatively share spiritual truths and insights that can make the world a better place.

Here are some examples of participants discovering their inner purpose:

Laura's story

Laura discovered her inner purpose in a manner she never expected. She learned she was serving her purpose in a way she had never understood. She had moved East to help her elderly mother to stay in her own home. After her mother passed, she remained in the area because of her position in the company. She let her manager know she wanted to go back West, but there were no open positions in the company at the time, so she stayed.

As she went through the P3 program, she discovered her internal purpose was to help people realize the unity of the world, that we are all closely connected, and our words and actions have immediate impact. She became aware she could do that anywhere and reclaimed her life and passion.

Her attitude improved but she still longed to return to the West. She considered moving and looking for a new job but did not want to jeopardize the salary and position she had worked for years to achieve.

One day, seemingly out of the blue, her manager asked if she was interested in moving back to Colorado. This opportunity resulted from her focus on her purpose and renewed passion for her work. A position magically seemed to open once she began working rooted in her integrated purpose. She took the new position, which was also a promotion.

The power of working from your integrated purpose cannot be overemphasized. Performing with the whole purpose is like strapping a jetpack to your back. It can propel you in ways you could never imagine.

Marsha's Story:

Marsha had been selling real estate for a number of years but was also interested in green building. Her external purpose was to help people buy and sell their houses with less stress and help them make good decisions. The month after she completed the P3 program she did a million dollars in real estate sales. She also got involved in the green building initiative. She discovered her inner purpose was to save the planet—one transaction at a time.

She participated in programs to bring awareness to green building features in homes. Her efforts began in the Raleigh, North Carolina, region. The first was a project to add these features to the Multiple Listing Service (MLS) listing for homes so that buyers could see the added value, which had not been documented previously. Following that, she created and co-created programs to educate realtors and later adjusters about how to integrate these green features into the sales process and adjustment reports. Marsha was awarded the 2009 Green Advocate of the Year from NC Green and the *Triangle Business Journal*. She also helped set up the green aspects of MLS in Wilmington and Southern Pines, and the initiative continues to spread.

A pioneer, she has extended her purpose and passion into an additional project and is one of the founders and drivers in a company that is having an even larger environmental impact that dwarfs what she did in real estate. Marsha is an example of someone who is living in her personal brand.

OUTER PURPOSE

What you accomplish in your life, your job and career form your outer purpose. It determines your roles and influences what others think of you. These are considered what you traditionally call *goals*.

This process begins when you make choices about what you like in school. You determine your educational ambitions, your major in school or industry, what type of work you want to do, and how you plan to attain your career goals. If you start your own company, instead of pursuing the path to the perfect position, you plan how to structure your business so you can create the ideal enterprise. These choices are the foundation for financial goals.

Your financial goals flow out of:

- The income you want
- When you want to retire
- Your desired car
- The house you want to live in
- Your desire to travel
- Savings to retire or begin another endeavor

You also set goals for family and for friends. Although these tend to be developed after your educational and financial objectives, they are important as well.

- Will you get married and when?

- What kind of friends do you want?

- What will you be doing at 20, 40, 60 and beyond?

- What legacy do you want to leave?

Many people define themselves through their jobs and careers: I am a doctor, an engineer, healthcare worker, a marketer, etc. Your job takes a significant amount of time in your life. Therefore, you may see yourself as an extension of your work and this makes sense—until you lose that job or encounter a dramatic life change. You base a large portion of your self-concept in this external purpose.

The next way you define yourself from the outside is through your roles. You are a mother, father, sibling, boss, employee, helper… The list goes on. Your roles are one of the most comfortable ways you think of yourself.

It is interesting that when families get together, siblings seem to revert to acting as they did when they were growing up. Those roles are so strongly ingrained that you can slip back into them naturally.

In your working environment, you fall into business roles as boss, employee, manager, executive or worker. Moving from an employee into a management role often creates challenges for you and others because relationships with those who were peers cannot stay the same within the company situation. Entrepreneurs experience this when hiring friends. Changes in roles demand that your previous associations be examined and may need to be modified. In either case, there is often pain in these adjustments. Very few people are prepared to work in a truly non-hierarchical organization where roles are disregarded.

One of the subtler ways you define yourself is through how others see you. You were probably programmed to worry about what others think of you. This quality in itself is mostly beneficial because it creates a moral framework and allows you to develop empathy. If you can put yourself in someone else's shoes and look at yourself, you can understand and appreciate how others feel. Without empathy, life is shallow. However, an unintended consequence of this thinking can be an obsession with how others perceive you. There's an old joke that people worry about what others think of them when actually others aren't thinking about them at all. This saying underlines the relative lack of importance of your concern about what others think of you. We will examine perception in a later chapter.

All these factors are useful in defining your outer purpose. When I consider people with highly recognizable outer purposes, I think of modern champions: Martin Luther King Jr., John F. Kennedy, Abraham Lincoln, Mother Teresa, Nelson Mandela, Jonas Salk.

You could feel the energy behind the purpose of these people when they spoke and even today long after they have left us. It is reflected in their writing, photos, in videos and audio recordings as well as articles written about them.

The outer purpose concerns your social status and what you want to have in your life, especially the material things. These are the "*Do*" considerations. When thinking about the future, your purpose is reflected in how you are perceived. Will you be a leader in your community, at work or in a group, or would you rather operate behind the scenes? Will you innovate? Is your intent to first and foremost provide for your family and enjoy the weekends with them? Are you driven to excel in a company or push your own enterprise to new heights, or do you labor from 9 to 5 and then achieve your purpose elsewhere?

Some want to be rich or famous. The drive to be known or well-to-do will direct someone in a different direction from the desire to help others. Although you may be able to do all these simultaneously, one of them will be the primary *driver* and may exclude others.

Considering these roles, I have designated 12 external roles people strive towards:

1. Initiator

2. Communicator

3. Leader

4. Diplomat

5. Explorer

6. Innovator

7. Gatherer

8. Nester

9. Enhancer

10. Detective

11. Manager

12. Producer

EXERCISE 7 YOUR EXTERNAL ROLES

One or more of these external roles should resonate with you immediately as you read through the list of descriptions. People often fall into more than one of these categories, but the important point is to see which ones apply to you and others around you. Knowing this about yourself helps to determine your outer purpose. This also helps you to understand how to stay true to your purpose in the work you do.

Read the definitions of each of these to determine which are your top three. Write these three roles on a sheet of paper or on the Roles exercise sheet.

(1) Initiators: You might be an initiator if you are motivated by starting a number of companies, projects and activities. You usually have multiple ventures going on simultaneously and enjoy the diversity and opportunity to move from one to another as you see fit. You are perceived as a go-getter and have immense amounts of energy. The outer purpose is easy to observe for initiators. You often have difficulties completing what you start and will team up with others for full productivity or may leave many projects unfinished.

(2) Communicators: If you are a teacher, speaker, coach or counselor, this may be your role. Your ability to express ideas and share solutions uniquely qualifies you to work as a connector between various people and you may be in a position of translating between different members of a team. For instance, you may fill a role of liaison between the designer and engineer and the engineer and the manufacturer. To be effective, you must be good listeners as well as a good speaker to excel in your work.

(3) Leaders: This might be you if you serve in an official position such as a CEO, CFO, CTO or hold a position as a project manager or another lead in a company or corporation. However, you do not have official titles or positions; you may take on leadership tasks informally. In a group, you may be the *real* leader to whom others go when they need a problem solved rather than the official designate. You naturally assume your roles when something is needed, and you can fill that need. Great leaders can inspire and motivate others who follow. Some of you do this naturally with charisma while others are excellent at planning and structuring to make it easy for others to work with you.

(4) Diplomats: If your mode of working with people is to reduce conflict between or among folks, this could be you. You look for and present solutions where compromises can help all parties to achieve their goals. You often work as a mediator to offer resolutions that none of the conflicted parties could discover on their own. You are also skilled at seeing things in common amongst the parties that they cannot see for themselves.

(5) Explorers: Are you on the lookout for something new and exciting? As an explorer, you are a thrill seeker and hungry for new experiences. You will be the first to try new products, activities and ventures, especially where there is high-risk involved. You may also be leaders and encourage others to follow in the pursuit of your explorer actions.

(6) Innovators: If you look for the newest trend, products or processes in terms of creating something novel, you might be an innovator. You are forever restless and looking for a newer or better way to do something. Your innovations often come from your own frustration with how things are done currently, and this feeds a desire to provide a better way, product or service. You love generating ideas but may not be adept at bringing these into manifestation. You may rely on others to do so.

(7) Gatherers: Do you seek to acquire? You might become a found objects artist or a collector of coins or antique cars or Barbie dolls. In any case, you are interested in preserving objects or more intangible ideas of the past or present. You like to share your finds or collections with others. One gatherer I know is an e-Bay expert and teaches other gatherers to use that platform. He is constantly on the lookout for collectables of all types and has become a resource for those around him who want to sell things that others no longer deem relevant.

(8) Nesters: This may be you if you like to stay close to home and create a perfect environment. When you travel, you do the same thing in groups. If that describes you, you are a nester. You like to entertain at home and usually are a member of groups of similar-minded persons. When you see folks attending an event together or camping together, there is a high probability that these are nesters out for their activity.

(9) Enhancers: If you have a hankering to build a better mousetrap or make a richer coconut cream pie, this is you. You strive to improve something in your environment. Some of you are engineers; others are chefs or inventors. What differentiates you from innovators is that you improve products or processes that already exist rather than coming up with new ones. Investors, financial advisors, accountants and coaches also fit into this role as you help others and/or yourselves to increase personal worth or capabilities. An enhancer's goals pertain to improving or perfecting what is around you.

(10) Detectives: If you are one of those people who love to solve puzzles and dig for answers below the surface, you fit into the detective category. You see the world as a mysterious place waiting to have you uncover solutions to unanswered questions. You may be writers or psychologists. Great marketers mine the deeper reaches of the mind or look for motives to purchase or act. You may be searching philosophical principles for truths or digging deeply into an event to get the real story. Often reporters or freelance writers, you are adept at asking the right questions at the right time.

(11) **Managers:** Do you excel at getting projects completed and helping people to utilize their highest potential? You may be a manager. An additional characteristic is that you usually have a more limited scope of duties than leaders and are responsible for smaller teams. When you are an effective manager, you are able to encourage those who work for you to achieve their goals concurrently with the larger objectives of the group. You will remove roadblocks and offer advice. You have experience in the domain of helping others perform. Successful managers do not take people through a step-by-step process but instead set direction and let them determine how the work will be done.

(12) **Producers:** Those who are producers play a critical role that deals with implementing what another has imagined. You bring projects to fruition by doing what needs to be done to actualize the idea. You often work for managers (but could work independently as a consultant) and are vital for initiators and innovators.

GWEN'S ANSWER:

Communicator, Detective, Enhancer

Unfortunately, you may not have not found the perfect employment in which to perform your role. I often hear people say that they are under-utilized in a job, and I have felt that way myself. This can indicate that you are working in a position (or have taken on a role) that is not aligned to your purpose. This type of dissatisfaction can cause you to move to another job. If you shift from one job to another, never finding a good fit, you might be ignoring your basic roles or settling for positions that do not match your inner or outer purpose.

Understanding your outer purpose can help align you with the kind of work you are suited for in the workplace as well as in organizations and clubs.

Once the inner and outer purposes have been discovered, it is time to integrate them.

I suggest you take a break here to let the previous exercises swirl around in your mind.

INTEGRATED PURPOSE

What is most interesting to me is that the inner purpose, while often not articulated, is reflected in the outer purpose. Although you may not know your inner purpose, it actually drives the outer one.

A teacher may say that her purpose is to educate better than her teachers did and to provide a better experience for students. That is the outer purpose, but what might the inner purpose be? Did she see inequitable treatment of some students by adults based on what they thought these students could do? When she was a student, was she bored and ready to tune out? Did she realize she would squander her potential in such an environment, prompting a desire to prevent others from making the same mistake? Did she admire a good teacher and want that same attention? Each of these situations would be a foundation for a different inner purpose. Each of these outer purposes, although they might appear to be the similar, would be significantly different.

A female executive might say that her purpose is to make money. Her inner purpose might stem from being raised in a deprived environment and wanting to provide more for her family. Or maybe she wants to be completely self-reliant. Perhaps she wants to be sure she has control of her life, unlike her parents, whom she watched struggling as she grew up.

In *The Great Gatsby*, Gatsby's success seems to come from his outer purpose: the desire to become wealthy and to flaunt his richness. We watch him throw opulent parties and invite all the A-list people. It is only later in the book that we realize his inner purpose is to be accepted by those with traditional wealth, specifically the woman he loves who has married a blue blood from the upper class. This revelation is helpful in seeing the difference between inner and outer purpose.

Many authors' outer purposes center around selling books. Their inner purposes, however, could vary significantly. You might be seeking fame or have a burning desire to inform people about something you have discovered. Did you have a life experience that could help others? Do you want to entertain? Is your inner purpose to motivate people to take action in a certain way in their families or communities?

Speakers usually feel they have something to share that they want to communicate in person (outer purpose). Your inner purpose might be parallel to those of authors or might be instructional to help people live more productive lives. You may know that sharing your story could help others avoid difficulties you have had to overcome, or you might want to teach a specialized skill so that audience members can progress in their careers.

Melding together the inner and outer purpose creates a powerful presentation for authors and speakers. By understanding this meshing of the inner and outer, you are able to set yourself apart from other authors and speakers and even those who work with the same subject matter.

When you find this alignment, you may find yourself accomplishing things you only dreamed of in the same way Marsha has. Your dreams will be supercharged when you are driven by an integrated purpose. With your conscious mind and your unconscious mind aligned, you can achieve remarkable things.

SUMMARY

Purpose is the reason to be who you are and do what you do in this life.

When contemplating purpose, think of it as having an outer and inner component. The outer purpose can be discovered by an examination of external factors in the environment. The inner purpose evolves from the self-discovery process. The first is aligned with utility, the second with passion.

Values are the concepts you live by and that you promote in the outside world. You can discover your values by talking with a close friend who can provide the reflection you need or do it alone.

No one can tell you your inner purpose; you must discover it from within. The nature of inner purpose, however, does not mean that you cannot get help in finding it, only that you must be willing to explore and have the desire to open this treasure.

Being activities bring you back to yourself.

What you accomplish in your life, your job and career form your outer purpose.

Doing activities involve the external roles you play and how others see you.

Although you may not know your inner purpose, it actually drives the outer purpose.

Chapter 4

The Purpose-Passion Connection

The challenge, then, is to marry the inner and outer purpose in an authentic, comfortable and conscious way. What is authentic? How can you make your combined purpose conscious?

In the branding sense, authenticity is sharing who you are in a direct, approachable and engaging way. In the next part of the book, I will delve into this principle since it is one of the cornerstones of a personal brand.

To be effective you must be comfortable in your own skin and with how you present yourself. When grounded in your personal brand, authentically crafted, you project a confident and pleasing *version* of who you are.

Creating a conscious image allows you to spotlight your skills, abilities and values to better offer your service to others. This architecting of an authentic image is covered later in the book.

Let's get a head start on the process. To become conscious of the true self and purpose, ask and answer *The Big Three Questions*.

The Big Three are:

- Who am I?
- What am I meant to do?
- Who can I serve?

WHO AM I?

Let's tackle the first question. To answer this question, you begin with the excavation of passions described in Exercises 1, 2 and 3. Once you have completed the list of passions from childhood and adulthood and compared those that are still relevant, you can get a preliminary picture of yourself.

Each person has a unique matrix of characteristics, a distinct combination cobbled together in his or her own specific way. You will complete that as you build your brand in Part IV.

WHAT AM I MEANT TO DO?

What exactly does this question convey? What is the meaning of *meant to do*? This concept deals with alignment to your integrated passion-purpose. It is often an iterative (repeated more than once) process to figure out what you are actually supposed to do. In a sense, it is like determining the right paint color for a room. I am sure I am not alone in having painted a room only to realize the hue is not exactly right. When painting our kitchen, my wife and I went through three shades of yellow-tan before settling on the right one. The first coat we put on the whole room only to realize it was so bright that we were not comfortable cooking there. When we applied the second color, we did only part of a wall and found it looked muddy. Re-applying paint for the third time, we had a color that matched our vision. Although it took three tries, the last one was perfect.

Like our journey in selecting the correct color, finding exactly what you are meant to do may be a process of trial and error, *and that is good!* As I look back at my career, I experienced the following positions and roles:

- Public high school teacher
- Public middle school teacher
- Substitute teacher
- Poet
- Cab driver
- Restaurant worker (waiter, prep cook, greeter)/Bartender
- Software trainer
- Technical writer
- Business owner
- Business coach
- Writing coach
- Course designer
- Freelance writer
- Marketing writer
- Personal brand workshop producer and presenter
- Social media content writer
- Author, speaker
- Publisher

In each of these positions, I learned skills and found different types of fulfillment. I grew into all of these roles, but like a jacket that didn't quite fit or that coat of paint that wasn't quite right, I found something in each experience that was a nearer match and led me closer to what I was supposed to do.

My current and best-fitting role is as a writer, publisher for independent writers, non-fiction mentor and personal branding architect. My circuitous path led to what I was meant to do. I have met people who knew from the start what they wanted and became that; I had to organically create the role I desired to play.

I find it interesting that many of the people who participated in the P3 program thought they were on their path until they realized what they were doing was not what they were *meant to do*. The longer these people thought they were satisfied, the more courage it took to look at alternatives. My father worked for 40 plus years in essentially the same profession and never considered anything else because his primary focus was to provide for his family. The following generations have been more fortunate, and we have sought out work that is aligned to who we are.

As you think about your best fit for what you are meant to do, you may have to go through a few versions of re-creating yourself. Be patient, follow up on as many opportunities as you can, and remember you can start this process at any age. There are those who were ready to ask this question and pursue the answers only after retirement.

If you are having trouble determining the answer to this question, you may want to work on the next question and return to this one afterward.

WHO AM I HERE TO SERVE?

Based on your answers of who you are and what you are meant to do (if you have completed this), you can respond to this third question.

Some of you are considering the question of service in order to answer the previous question; all are closely intertwined.

Ask yourself who can you help along their path to better understand who you are meant to serve. Does your mission focus on children, adults, retirees? Men, women or both? Do you want to work with corporate people, entrepreneurs, stay-at-home moms or those in job transition? Think about where you can make the most impact and what would create the greatest fulfillment for you.

One way to approach this is to find out what problem you are solving whether through your books, speaking, consulting or other services you provide. When you work with others what do you want them to achieve? Your offering, whether coaching or done-for-you work (a turnkey solution for clients), has value. If you know what that value is, you can hone in on whom you can best serve.

When most people start a new business, they take any client or customer who will employ them. This is only natural and is the way most businesses begin. When I first opened my marketing business, we had a diversity of clients and tried to serve everyone. If there was a job to do and we didn't know exactly how to do it, one of us would go learn how to do what was needed so we could deliver the desired results. We were somewhat successful doing this and this strategy increased our offerings. There were two problems we encountered: First, it took a lot of time to understand customers in new markets and gain the necessary skills, and, secondly, we did slip up a few times and failed. We either returned their fee or found another way to compensate them since reputation is key to any business.

We were concerned that we would not survive by limiting the scope of our offerings and the kind of clients we wanted to serve. We reluctantly narrowed our offerings to those things we already knew how to deliver and something amazing happened. As soon as we determined this and who we wanted to serve, we found the kind of work and clients we were seeking. This was a big realization for us; we had come from a corporate environment where we had no control over customers, clients or the work requested.

It took repeated experiences, however, to practice this lesson in earnest. As the leader of my company, I often chased other things I thought would create more profit. I had the *shiny object syndrome* and only after I observed it in another business associate did I recognize it. We would begin with great successes, and it looked like the best direction to go, but after a time we would find ourselves again diluting our offerings and be unable to articulate a clear message about what we did. Our delivery of these services was also not efficient.

EXERCISE 8 WHO AM I MEANT TO SERVE?

To determine your clientele, consider a few things.

1. Determine your reach. If your reach is highly personal, it might be in your immediate neighborhood. You might be thinking a little larger and include friends and others in your local area. If your reach is wider, where do you want to work—in your state or province—or do you want to be national? Some people supply services internationally through technology like teleseminars and virtual conferences. With the internet available, your scope can expand to incorporate a worldwide audience.

   Figure out *where you will do your work* and where those you serve are located. How much you are willing to travel, which modes of transportation you will use and cost factors are part of the equation. How will you keep profitable when you spend hours a day driving to prospect meetings? There is a dilemma here: Spending a bulk of time and money going to and from meetings is not productive, but neither is waiting for clients. Prospecting is expensive, however, without prospecting you have no clients and no money.

My reach is _____.

2. Next consider *how you will communicate* with customers and clients. If you are local, you will have the opportunity to meet face to face. Even with local relationships, the phone, email, social media or conference calls may be more efficient. Your communication choices will factor into how you work with others and how you can most efficiently spend your time. Sometimes a face-to-face meeting is more productive and worth the travel time and expense, especially at the beginning of a project.

Connection methods: _____

3. What kinds of clients do you want? What is their sex and age? What interests do they have? Where do they hang out?

Describe your client: _____

4. How many clients do you need? It may be easier to work with just a few clients than a larger number. Bigger clients allow you to focus more on their tasks rather than having to juggle multiple projects. With many small clients, the danger is that each may take a lot of time to communicate and this may make it unprofitable.

How many clients do you need per week? _____ per month? _____ per year? _____

Drew Becker

For writers and speakers, these questions are modified.

1. Determine your reach. Who do you want to read your book? Is your book personal and meant only for your immediate or extended family? I have produced family histories that are intended for members of a family. You might be thinking a little larger and include friends and others in your local area, but if your reach is wider, where do you want to promote the book. Will you do readings in your city, state or province or do you want to be national? With the internet available, your scope can easily extend internationally.

    Where do you want to speak? The same questions apply. For most successful speakers, travel is required to increase their reach.

    Your Reach: _____ Venues: _____

2. Next consider *how you will communicate* with customers and clients. If you are local, you have the opportunity to meet them in person—perhaps at a book release, a reading or at a venue where you speak. Even with local relationships, tele-events, webinars, email, social media or conference calls may be useful. Sometimes a face-to-face meeting is more productive and worth the travel time and expense, especially for speakers who are securing a venue and for authors who can sell their books directly.

    Communication Methods: _____

3. Who would appreciate experiencing your speaking or want to read your book? Which people will your topic engage? Think about gender, age group(s), work, interests, hobbies and other ways to identify your audience.

   Describe your audience: _____

4. How many readers or what size audiences do you want to reach?

   How many readers or size of audiences? _____

GWEN'S ANSWERS:

1. As a writer, I would be thinking small not to seek a worldwide audience. Getting the word out about the work will happen locally and online. Teleseminars can reach a wide audience, and I'm willing to offer in-person events locally and regionally with occasional travel to more distant places as needed.

2. I've done many teleseminars through the years and certainly will continue. I will offer a local book release and signings and readings regionally with potential travel to other locations as opportunities become available.

3. My work appeals to open-minded, spiritual people who are seeking enlightening entertainment (for the novels) or helpful information (for the non-fiction). My audience is comprised of seekers, people who are awakening to the more spiritual side of life, and those who believe in or are open to the idea of realms beyond the physical world we see. The vast majority of this audience thus far seem to

be female with a wide age range (early 20s to 70s). Teenagers often are attracted to my work as well and frequently find out about it from their mothers. People who work in the healing arts or delve into this as a hobby are drawn to my writing. Artists and others who are creative are among my audience as well. My audience tends to be interested in intuition, angel cards, and spiritual adventures including meditation.

4. Right now my readership is in the hundreds, but my goal is to reach hundreds of thousands (or more).

With an understanding of integrated purpose, you have completed the ground work for the rest of the process. You are now ready to get a deeper look into what a personal brand is in Part II.

Summary

The challenge is to marry the inner and outer purpose in an authentic, comfortable and conscious way.

The Big Three questions are:

- **Who am I?**
  You have a unique matrix of characteristics, a distinct combination cobbled together in your own specific way.

- **What am I meant to do?**
  As you think about your best fit for what you are meant to do, you may have to go through a few versions of re-creating yourself.

- **Who can I serve?**
  What problem are you solving? When you work with others, what do you want them to achieve? Your offering has value and, if you know what that value is, you can hone in on whom you can best serve.

PART II

YOUR PERSONAL BRAND

To find yourself, think for yourself.
          —Socrates

We move around in our autonomy
Encased so willingly in our anatomy.
          —Drew Becker

Part II presents many of the concepts necessary to architect your brand throughout the rest of the book. I have covered the difference between branding and personal branding. This knowledge is critical in understanding the components of a personal brand. You must also understand your authenticity, distinctiveness and notability.

Chapter 5

Your Personal Brand

As stated earlier, brands and personal brands are all around us. To work on your brand, you need to become aware of other brands and their pervasive nature, which are taken for granted by most people but which have a strong psychological effect.

WHAT ARE THE COMPONENTS?

Personal branding has many components. These can be viewed in two categories: tangibles and intangibles. I explore the intangibles here and mention the tangibles, which will be addressed later when you flesh out your brand. Remember these are extensions of your unique and universal elements.

INTANGIBLES:

Let's examine the intangibles first since they are closely related to the passion and purpose exercises you have already completed. Your passion and purpose drive your personal brand and, along with these other intangibles, create the framework or blueprint for the brand itself.

Drew Becker

Your Promise

Nothing about your brand is more fundamental than the promise you make. This promise is not just for your clients and customers but extends to employees and stakeholders. It is the umbrella under which all the other components exist. None of these components should reside outside of the boundaries you establish with the promise. For example, if you had a film company, you would not want to make a brand promise for family-rated entertainment, then release films with excessive violence or strong sexual content. If you did, these films would work against your brand. The promise is not something you tout from the pinnacle of your website nor is it part of your elevator speech; most companies use it only as the underlying theme for their messages. It is usually not explicit. Your promise is *the* critical concept underlying all the other elements.

So what kind of promise is this? This pledge *encompasses* the customer experience you design. When someone engages you and your company, what do you want them to think and feel about the experience?

Here are some examples of brand promises:

- We provide family fun and adventure. —Disney
- Own the coolest, easiest to use, cutting edge technology. —Apple
- Access your library anywhere on multiple platforms. —Amazon Kindle
- Own the ultimate driving machine. —BMW
- Quiet luxury. Crafted experiences. Intuitive service. —Marriott
- Your package will get there overnight. Guaranteed. —FedEx
- Enjoy endless play. —Lego
- Daily inspiration. —Starbucks

78

A few of these promises are actually used in their messaging or slogans, but most are internal to the companies and will not see the light of day in communications with the customers.

To realize the power of a promise that is not explicit, think about what the design for a phone might be if it were created by Lego. The first thing you would expect would be multiple bright colors. It might look like a transformer toy and the shape might be configurable. It would feature games and be interactive so that you could build a complete custom piece of technology.

What if a phone were designed by BMW? This would be sleek and have a shiny, easy-to-grip surface. It also would have advanced features no other manufacturer had produced.

The examples above are for corporate brands, but what does a promise for a personal brand look like? Michael Jordan's brand has to do with determination and practice. When you read his story, you understand that. His promise is evident in the film *Space Jam* in how he coaches his animated team. When you go to see a Jackie Chan movie, you know he will help the underdog. Even before the advent of personal brands, if you watched a Fred Astaire movie, you knew there would be elegant dancing.

Let me give you some more examples of promises from the rest of us non-celebrities:

- One of my associates, Brook, promotes herself as the caring coach, which is her promise.

- A financial planner, Remy, promises to guide you through the maze of investment with simple language.

- Author J.C. will help you discover North Carolina state history in chewable chunks.

- Tim will make your website "Google-icious."

- Jessica promises to create personalized and unique promotional items.

- Dori drums you to better health and productivity.

Values

You have already completed an exercise about values earlier, and now I want to dive deeper into their meaning and influence on your brand. What you stand for, believe in and act on make up your values. What do you want to be known for in the world? Does your brand inspire confidence in your authenticity, your sense of fair play, your desire to help others or your need to make a specific change in the world? What are the ideas that emerge from your passion and purpose?

Values can be defined as your principals, standards and behavioral code of conduct. Values are a reflection of an interior view of yourself. If someone could open up your head, these would be one of the first images they would perceive. Your values are shaped by your experiences and your environment, so they are basic to your sense of self. They reflect how you were raised and are often similar to those of your parents unless you reject your upbringing, which certain circumstances can foster. If there is trauma or deep pain in childhood, you might rebuild values as a reaction to those incidents.

Values are at work in everything you consciously do and many of your unconscious actions. They are so ingrained that you often overlook them and their influence on you; however, be assured your values are instigating your behavior.

Some people cannot stand idly by in the face of injustice and are prompted to act. Others may not even register these incidents or may not even perceive them. This blindness is also a value. Those who ignore others around them or only see them as a means to an end are also expressing a value.

Sometimes values can be overrun by fears. You may know what you should do, but because of your concerns, you do nothing or join in with others whose values are antithetical to yours. Even in these cases, your values are at work since you may feel disgrace or disgust with yourself after the fact.

Your values are an integral part of your brand.

From values, let's look at something a bit more accessible to discover. Most companies and corporations spend time and money to discover their mission and vision. A personal brand can also have a mission and vision to help guide you. Let us begin by defining mission, then vision.

Mission

Mission or a mission statement is a declaration of purpose. It is necessary to write it down because it is easy to believe you have defined it when all you have is a general idea in mind. Since we have already addressed purpose, it is a short step to writing a mission statement. This statement sets a direction for your brand that may include who you are meant to serve.

The mission is something to be accomplished, so it details what your brand will do in the world.

Here are a few examples of mission statements from companies you may be familiar with:

- Jet Blue: In the air and on the ground, we're committed to bettering the lives of our customers, crewmembers and communities—and inspiring others to do the same.

- Patagonia: Build the best product, cause no unnecessary harm, use business to inspire and implement solutions to the environmental crisis.

- Amazon: We seek to be Earth's most customer-centric company for four primary customer sets: consumers, sellers, enterprises, and content creators.

- AT&T: We connect people with their world, everywhere they live and work, and do it better than anyone else.

- Burt's Bees: We make people's lives better every day—naturally.

- Google: We organize the world's information and make it universally accessible and useful.

- Hallmark: Make the world a more caring place by helping people laugh, love, heal, say thanks, reach out and make meaningful connections with others.

- Nike: We bring inspiration and innovation to every athlete in the world.

- TED: Support the ideas and perspectives of brilliant creators and innovators.

- Virgin Atlantic: We embrace the human spirit and let it fly.

Some people do not trust corporate mission statements and think they are marketing ploys; however, I believe they set a standard for employees and management to live up to. Your personal mission should be down to earth and easy for you to understand and pursue.

Vision

Vision or a vision statement is a declaration of what a company wants to achieve. It is a future view of where the company will be or, in the case of a person, where you want to be. Like a mission statement, it is usually written. These are usually mid or long-term goals. Here are some examples of vision statements from famous companies:

- Amazon: Create a future of global dominance in the online retail industry.

- AT&T: We aspire to be the most admired and valuable company in the world. Our goal is to enrich our customers' personal lives and to make their businesses more successful by bringing to market exciting and useful communications services, building shareowner value in the process.

- Hallmark: We will be the company that creates a more emotionally-connected world by making a genuine difference in every life, every day.

- Nike: We envision being the number one athletic company in the world.

- TED: We support the ideas and perspectives of brilliant creators and innovators. (This is the same as their mission.)

- Virgin Atlantic: Safety, security and consistent delivery of the basics are the foundations of everything we do. The success of our three-year strategy requires us to build on these foundations by focusing on the business and leisure markets and driving efficiency and effectiveness.

Messaging

Your foundational message must be powerful and is the cornerstone for your brand communication. Once you have polished your mission, vision and promise and understand your passion and purpose, you can begin building your messaging. All your messages must be clear and grounded in your brand.

Your foundational message is an anchor from which all your tangibles are created. This includes:

- All the images you use
- Stories you tell
- Materials you produce and distribute
- Your website
- All the other tangibles of your personal brand

Use this message as a basis to create communications for each campaign, social media post, press release, new offering and everything else you will build to support your brand.

TANGIBLES

How people first encounter your brand is critical to your success. The visible pieces of your brand create a first impression, so you should carefully plan these based on the intangible components.

The tangible parts of your brand connect the intangibles already described with the outside world and are the vehicle to broadcast your brand outward. The tangibles are detailed in a later chapter, but here is a list of them to help you see where we are going.

These components are:

- Logo and graphics
- Message
- Tagline
- Website
- Video
- Email

- Social Media
- Collateral Materials
- Telephone answering script
- Image

BUILDING YOUR PERSONAL BRAND

The original name for the *Purpose Powered Process* was *Your Essential DNA*. The acronym DNA stood for distinct, notable and authentic, and these three concepts are at the heart of a personal brand. An examination of these aspects of personal brands creates a foundation for the work.

AUTHENTICITY

The ancient Greek aphorism, "Know thyself," was inscribed at the Temple of Apollo in Delphi. This meaningful maxim has become a cliché that is even more popular today with the authenticity trend. The term authenticity *has devolved into a buzzword*. It has a watered-down meaning and is overused. Part of the reason for this is that what it takes to be authentic begins with self-examination, which is a step often skipped.

But don't you already know yourself? This fact is counterintuitive since you do have self-awareness. But self-awareness is not self-knowledge. Self-knowledge is not easy to come by. To achieve an understanding of yourself, you must do some self-analysis and contemplation as well as have feedback from outside. The necessity of combining both types of knowledge can be challenging.

So, to get beyond the trite usage of *authenticity*, you must begin by understanding what it is in its essence. Authenticity is being and then acting as *the real you*. What that means is that you are willing to share *some* of your personal life but not all. Later in the book, I will examine techniques to realize your personal brand based on your authenticity. There are many avenues to express your authenticity. Some of these are face-to-face meetings, through social media, video, dress and accessories, and by telephone. These avenues are actually vehicles to articulate the personal brand.

What does your authentic personal brand look like when it is built? A successful brand enables you to (1) operate from awareness, (2) respond in the present, (3) measure reality, (4) act in accordance with your brand and (5) communicate with intention.

Operate from Awareness

With your personal brand intact, you understand yourself and your services and products which allows you to plan your actions. This doesn't mean you can't be spontaneous; it means your spontaneity is rooted in awareness of who you are. Those who fail to create a personal brand will be defined by those around them. You can control how you are perceived by others by carefully planning and crafting your personal brand. If your actions, words and personal presentation are not planned or at least considered, and you are flying by the seat of your pants, you cannot expect your brand to represent you. However, if you know how you want to be seen, you can architect your brand and actions to create that impression.

Respond in the Present

It is interesting how often we can forget to be *present*. Instead of concentrating on what's right in front of us, our minds drift as we think of the next meeting or what items we left off our grocery list. Especially with the distraction of cell phones and social media, it takes discipline to ignore the urge to check for messages or the next post.

Most cell phone users are addicted to the constant pinging sounds emitted by their devices. Splitting your attention between your surroundings and electronic devices blocks the ability to operate from that personal brand perspective and focus your attention on those around you and the task at hand.

Driving is another activity where some people are multi-tasking and not paying attention. That driver who switches lanes at the last minute is distracted, often thinking ahead to the next activity or talking on the cell or even eating and drinking while operating the vehicle.

What is important to remember in terms of personal brand is that when you are distracted, you cannot be thinking about your image or the person with whom you are interacting.

Measure Reality

Take into account who you are with and where you are; relate to the reality around you when articulating your personal brand. Presenting your personal brand is not necessarily a straightforward activity. You must consider which part of the brand is most appropriate in your current situation. A full personal brand is singular in purpose but manifold in execution. How can your personal brand augment what the person you are communicating with needs? By sizing up the situation, you will know how to impress without having to *show off*.

Act in Accordance with Your Brand

Your behavior is the strongest reflection of your brand. When one of the values of your brand is violated, you should feel a need to intervene and stand up for that value. Sometimes this may be excusing yourself from a situation and walking away; other times you may have to say something and let people know where you stand. Personal brands are not timid.

Communicate with Intention

When you respond to someone, be aware of intention. This begins with meaningful listening and continues with intentional articulation. Listening skills include knowing what you are listening for as well as hearing the words. Decide what you want to achieve in a conversation or interaction. This may seem inauthentic, but upon reflection it is not. This decision is based on which part of your brand you want to articulate.

On occasion, I have been guilty of being more interested in getting my point across than whether the listener understood what I was trying to convey. This was not intentional—I was just so excited about what I was expressing that I got caught up in the moment. And that's the point; if I were intentional in my communication, I would stop to think how I could best explain my point from the listener's perspective as well as share the excitement.

I have met people in networking situations who are so impassioned about their product or service that they don't stop long enough to think about or ask if it has value for the other person. The overzealous salesperson may make a quick sale but rarely creates a long-term relationship. Selling one book is okay but selling yourself as an author or speaker can create a long-term stream of income from a potential client.

I was at a meeting recently talking to someone who attends regularly, and I shared writing events I was producing with him. Nothing in particular that I offered was of interest until he mentioned that he was doing interviews. I mentioned my book about interviewing and he was ready to buy. I did not have to sell it to him. He might purchase other books and products in the future. Up to that point in the conversation, I had not brought up my books. I rarely do so unless a book has just been released or it is relevant to the other person. Then, I find that they buy willingly, because the book interests them or they want to support me.

If your brand includes helping people, be sure you have sharpened listening skills; you must understand the problem before assisting others with a solution or offering advice.

I am reminded of a business coach I know. Bill holds a monthly gathering in the area. He makes a point of meeting as many of the guests as he can and connecting them with someone else at the event. Although he fulfills his hosting duties well, he also finds a way to create valuable conversations. I have watched Bill give 15 minutes of business advice when he talks to someone. He seeks out someone he hasn't met before or spends time with people who know him and want to ask him a business question. In addition, he gives away one seat to his paid seminar. He invites interest in his workshop without selling it at all. Whenever I go to one of his events, I know there is a great possibility I will meet someone I can help or who can help me to increase business. Bill's personal brand is contagious, and those who are there pick up on the theme of helping one another. The awareness and purpose this coach brings to the event sets the tone for all the participants.

DISTINCTIVENESS

To be distinct is to be differentiated from others, to be recognizable as someone unique, to be unmistakable. One of the benefits of a strong personal brand is that you stand out in the marketplace. What you do best can spotlight you. This is the concept of *the hedgehog* presented by Jim Collins in *Good to Great*. Collins suggests that you find what you do better than anyone else and build on that. Become known for that one thing that you do best, and you will attract the right people. Of course, you have to offer value as well, often by giving a portion of your knowledge away.

When I think of sports figures like LeBron James, Michael Jordan or Steph Curry, I do not confuse them with anyone else. Each has carved out his own niche in basketball. Each has achieved celebrity status and is very conscious of his brand. The same is true for celebrity rock stars and movie actors.

In the same way, Tennessee Williams and August Wilson (who wrote the play and the Academy Award-winning movie *Fences*) have created works that marked their places in the world of drama. J. K. Rowling has not only crafted unique characters and multiple bestselling books and movies based on them but has built a prominent brand. Even though the Harry Potter book series ended after the seventh, she has written another successful novel, not related to the first. People flocked to purchase the new book because of her brand. Expanding her brand has allowed her to build an enterprise.

Others with distinct brands include Beyonce, Martha Stewart, Will Smith, Richard Branson and author Seth Godin. Many politicians rely on strong personal branding for their ability to draw votes.

Stories about distinction in personal branding abound. Oprah used her brand to build an empire. If she is connected to any event or product, it reflects her brand. She has one of the most prominent world brands, and her distinctness is a vital pillar for it.

However, you do not have to be a celebrity to build a distinct personal brand. What you need to do is determine what it is you want to be known for and provide value in that arena. You all know people who distinguish themselves by being the first to offer help when you are in need or who are open with advice when asked. You also know those who are tight-fisted with all their resources, and that makes them distinct as well. Be sure you are distinguishing yourself in the way you want to be perceived. Otherwise, you may be regarded in a non-flattering light.

There are those who can create a rough or curmudgeon persona and use it successfully. I have one friend whom I appreciate for his cynicism and sharp wit. He excels as a programmer but is a bit prickly. He has carved out a career due to his expertise but has challenges during his employment. I can count on him for a story about how the company he works with does absurd and counterproductive things. It connects me to my former corporate life and reminds me why I now own my own company. His personality is distinct but sometimes gets in his way as he pursues his career path.

Notability

Notability refers to being of note or noteworthy. A strong personal brand will establish you as someone who is worth the time to get to know. While being distinct indicates that you are different, being notable implies that you provide value to those you meet, and *they appreciate and tell others about you.* Designed notability is a key to activating your authenticity.

You can make yourself notorious but not notable. To become notorious, all you need to do is act outrageously and be sure others are watching and willing to spread their disgust, outrage or displeasure.

Others make you notable. People recognize you through your brand and want to talk about you and what you do. This is often the result of something you have done for them or an action that has benefited them such as an introduction to someone who has helped their business, family or friend.

Notability moves you into prominence. Notable people are in demand both on a personal level and in other venues such as the media. They are perceived as authorities. Notable people are quoted in newspapers, magazines, blogs and books. They appear on television and radio.

You can cultivate notability, but you cannot create it directly. It is the result of actions and behavior that you can craft. By knowing what you want to be known for, you can act both online and in person to support that.

The business coach I referred to is notable for helping entrepreneurs and business owners. In his conversations he asks people what is keeping them from getting to the next level in their businesses. He is generous with his time and is empathetic. His natural curiosity about others' businesses and his advice and understanding make him notable. He is well-known in the community and one of the first resources entrepreneurs seek out for counsel.

FROM DNA TO YOUR PERSONAL BRAND

The exercises presented in this book are derived from Genece's original program. These exercises enable you to define your authenticity, your distinctiveness and your notability.

To build the brand, you must go beyond the passion and purpose, but you will use those as building blocks. You already have a peek of what your personal brand might be. Completing more exercises will help you clarify this concept in the final section once you understand the underlying principles.

The benefit of an authoritative personal brand is that you become a purpose powered person or professional. You can expect a deep-rooted understanding that supports a powerful ability to present yourself, your business and your brand.

Summary

Personal Branding components can be intangible or tangible:

Intangible:

Your brand promise is what you are committed to deliver, and it acts as an the umbrella under which all the other components reside. None of these should reside outside of the boundaries you establish.

Values can be defined as your principals, standards and behavioral code of conduct. Values are a reflection of an interior view of yourself.

Your mission or a mission statement is a declaration of purpose.

Your vision statement is a declaration of what your company wants to achieve in the long run. It usually looks five years and beyond.

Your message must be powerful and is the cornerstone for your brand communications.

Tangibles are: *logo and graphics, messaging on print materials, tagline, website, video, email, social media, other collateral materials, answering script,* and *image.*

Authenticity is being and then acting as the real you. To do so you will: (1) operate from awareness, (2) respond in the present, (3) measure reality, (4) act in accordance with your brand and (5) communicate with intention.

Distinctiveness enables others to see you as unique. To do so, determine what it is you want to be known for and provide value in that arena.

Notability implies that you provide value to those you meet so they appreciate and tell others about you.

Others make you notable.

Chapter 6

Challenges to Your Personal Brand

WHAT ARE THE BARRIERS TO ARCHITECTING AND LIVING BY YOUR PERSONAL BRAND?

We live in a world that for many seems disjointed and antagonistic and is at odds with expressing your authentic self. Your passions and purpose can be obscured easily in the everyday bustle of living your life. Values connected with personal freedom conflict with what is broadcast day in and day out. The concept of freedom has been debased by advertisers and presented as the freedom to own the latest styles, buy the sleekest cars, sport novel hairstyles and communicate with the newest slang and emojis. These are all merely trends and are imitative.

As you grow up, you are caught between the idea of fitting in and standing out. Peer pressure to conform is enormous as you move into puberty and adolescence. The stigma of being different is exploitable by other teens and pre-teens who show distain for others in order to protect themselves. In those formative years, the fear of being called out, excluded or ridiculed is so strong that detrimental responses include becoming a bully or standing by as others are bullied rather than defending the object of the bullying. There are few contravening forces that can compete with this pressure.

The constraints to authenticity that you encounter daily fall into one of these categories:

- Restrictions to impress acceptable behavior
- Role rules you learn in regard to gender and relationships
- Peer pressure
- Acceptance based on fitting in
- Expectations of obedience

THE MASK OF YOUR PERSONALITY

I wrote this poem about the identity dilemma entitled *Mask:*

> Sculpted in familiar contour
> Life-controlled and so secure,
> It saves emotions from exploding
> Hidden for repair, I keep reloading.
>
> Worn in jest and subtle tact,
> It releases lies—it blocks react.
> We move around in our autonomy
> Encased so willingly in our anatomy.
>
> When in despair we try removal
> But it's secured by others' approval,
> Shatter, tear or smash we may
> We can't remove the face from clay.
>
> I scream from form to be set free
> But which is mask and which is me?
> © drew becker 1976

The difficulty with accepting these constraints is that eventually you may realize you have lost your joy and are no longer in touch with yourself. You have a choice to live in your uniqueness and feel that alignment every day. Once you reveal the face behind your mask, you can take the steps to live in your personal brand authentically and recover the enjoyment that has slowly eroded as you conformed to what others wanted, and you can make a living following your passions!

If you get discouraged during this process, a deeper look at these challenges might help to understand why. Use this knowledge to motivate you to stand up to external pressure or your own resistance. For more information see Appendix V.

Summary

We live in a world that for many seems disjointed and antagonistic and is at odds with expressing your authentic self.

The constraints to authenticity that you encounter daily fall into one of these categories:

- Restrictions to impress acceptable behavior
- Role rules you learn in regard to gender and relationships
- Peer pressure
- Acceptance based on fitting in
- Expectations of obedience

Once you reveal the face behind your mask, you can live in your personal brand authentically and recover the enjoyment while making a living following your passions!

Chapter 7

Perception, Language and Impact

Perception, language and impact all influence each other in your life and in building your personal brand.

You need to examine perception, language and impact to understand how the personal brand fits together. Let's begin with perception.

PERCEPTION

How you perceive the world will mold your language. Language can in turn change your perceptions and those of others as illustrated by examples of how using the wrong phrase or word can get a public figure in hot water and spread virally over the internet.

Language also influences your impact. Knowing and using the most effective words and phrasing helps to elicit the desired responses and is critical in becoming influential. Authors and speakers are keenly aware of this importance as are advertisers and marketers who spend a significant amount of time crafting messages to encourage buying behavior. The reverse is true as well; how many of you are impacted by penetrating language or have an advertising jingle or song run around in their heads?

Perception can influence impact because you choose your course of action to sway or convince others based on how you perceive them. Your impact also changes how you perceive them. Remember we like to do business with others we know, like and trust.

I recently spoke to a real estate agent and asked her about her brand. She replied with the company's mission. I asked some questions to delve into her personal brand. I questioned her about her passions, and, as she began to think and talk about these, she commented that this was like working with a psychoanalyst. I replied that there was a similarity because personal branding work relates to your values, abilities, likes and other questions you might explore to get a deeper understanding of yourself. She suddenly understood and commented that she hadn't thought too much about this but it interested her. She showed a willingness to move from unconscious to conscious. This willingness to explore is one of the first steps in increasing self-awareness and crafting a brand.

As you are architecting your brand, consider how you are perceived by others.

The building of a personal brand is a self-discovery process and a wonderful and enticing journey. You can gain an understanding of this process by completing the exercises in this book. Gaining knowledge about how you see the world around you is an important step.

How do you arrive at your perceptions of yourself and others? Perception is a complex idea, so let's look at a simple projection of it. Most people agree they are unique, but, if I ask them how they are unique, most give me a single characteristic (that they share with many others). You will see how to answer this question in upcoming exercises.

6

All of your communication and interaction rest on the foundation of perception. Perception works through your conscious and unconscious perspective.

For a more detailed look at perception, see Appendix II.

LANGUAGE

Eskimos have 50 words for snow. This reflects the importance of snow in their environment and the need to differentiate various qualities especially related to survival. This word diversity shows one example of how language is influenced by perception. In areas that rarely see snow, residents might only have one or a few words to describe the phenomena and the crystals that lie on the ground.

The labels we apply to other people can change what we see. What is the difference between a freedom fighter and a terrorist? A less extreme example is the name used by one political party for the other. In either case, using a word or phrase that conjures an image before the actual communication begins can set the tone for understanding or misunderstanding.

LEARNING LANGUAGE

We learn language. Then we used it to make sense of the world around us. We express our view of that world translating thoughts, emotions, insights and beneficial and detrimental feelings into words.

Humans are not born with language skills; vocabulary (the words we choose), grammar (the structure of how we form our sentences) and voice (inflection, speech patterns, speed, accent and more) are formed as we learn to speak. Later we acquire new ways to expand our expression.

Our earliest language was learned from our parents or those who raised us from birth. Beginning with our first words, our language is learned from listening and imitating. I remember saying things while young and one of my parents would ask, "Where did you hear that?" when those words and phrases were not part of our family linguistic style.

Of course, other major influences are books, movies and television. The mass media is a significant factor in our language development, and, for those children who spend more time watching television than interacting verbally with those around them, their speaking style will mirror mass media. One reason to find time to talk with young children is to compensate for the impact of mass media. With a balance, *your* values can be passed on instead of those espoused by television, video games and the web. This has critical importance when we differentiate ourselves and our brands.

The next linguistic influence is social and begins with children playing with other children and then entry into the educational system. During these years our classes (not only English) and classmates increase the vocabulary, modify grammar and impact voice. As children begin to read, they add to their linguistic style just as they have been doing consuming media.

POWER OF LANGUAGE

We use our words to influence others. They are powerful and can convey love and affection, can hurt, can heal and produce many different emotions in others. Because of this capacity, they are critical to your brand. Everything you say or write or communicate non-verbally is a reflection of your brand. After carefully crafting a brand, you need to pay attention to how you speak and be sure you are conveying the values and promises of your brand.

When I teach technical writing courses, I talk about modifying writing to reach the audience more effectively. The important element is that *this modification is a choice.* In the same way, what we communicate is the result of a series of choices about how we express ourselves. We are making a choice, conscious or unconscious, with all our words.

No one expects a person to parse every sentence and review every phrase before it is said. That would make communication a nearly insurmountable task. By being aware of your personal brand, your language will promote the concepts encapsulated in the brand. If integrity is a cornerstone of a brand, the speech will be as truthful as possible and there will be no intention to deceive. In addition, an effort will be made to assure that the message is understood as intended.

For a more detailed view of language, see Appendix III.

IMPACT

Who are the people you impact and how do you impact them? Some people have innate charisma and others seem to naturally follow them. Anyone can improve their influence once they understand what it is and how it operates.

Influence may be beneficial or detrimental. Like any other tool, it has a potential to be used either way. You can be assured that your impact will be positive when approaching influence with authenticity and good intentions. When your goal is to form a relationship for continued interaction rather than to influence someone once, your impact will be greater, and you have the potential to turn that person into a raving fan who will promote you in your community and theirs. Selling once to someone without building the relationship will yield only quick and usually non-repeatable profit.

Before I discuss more about influence, I would like to discuss a challenge that many of you may have had at one time or another in your lives: Losing your voice.

Losing My Voice

I know many people who have lost their voices. I don't mean literally, of course. I'm referring to the instances when you were intimidated or discouraged from speaking up. In fact, as children you were taught not to talk to strangers, but you need to be able to do this as an adult. When your voice is stolen, you often lose personal power as well. I learned this through my own experience.

I was reprimanded at an early age in school for speaking out of turn and was isolated from the class. I had to wear a sign that read, "Sit down and be quiet!" I understand that I was disruptive, but this had an unintended effect: I lost my voice for many years. I preferred to do projects on my own after that and only later reconditioned myself to participate. I felt as though whatever I had to say was less important than what others said. I would have to reclaim my voice, and, yet, I barely knew there was a problem.

Although I became an effective teacher and communicated excellently, that was a special situation. In that particular role, I had control of the communication. However, when among my non-teacher peers, I was often quiet. I realized I had not learned how to participate without either dominating or withdrawing. I was unsure of when to speak, so I often kept quiet and was comfortable with living with my lost voice. I have met others who share the domination/withdrawal coping mechanism. It may not be severe enough to prompt action because it is painful to recognize, but as time goes on that person usually realizes that his or her influence is being limited.

Something was missing but I did not know what I lacked. I could not transition from teaching to personal communicating. I did not realize it was because I had to give up personal control and lacked the confidence to participate on a level playing field.

Reclaiming the Voice

Once you realize that your persuasive abilities and your communication have been affected by past events, it is time to take action. First, try to recall what events were responsible for the detrimental effect on you. Identify the people involved and the feelings at that time. Then, begin to reconstruct your voice and your power.

You must reclaim your voice if it has been hijacked. To do this get rooted in your personal brand and spend time building your confidence through small steps. As you go through the exercises in this book, you will get a better sense of yourself, and you can use this to build a foundation to reclaim you voice and power.

Find opportunities you can succeed in influencing others and build on those. We mistakenly think all great speakers were born that way. If you ask successful speakers, you will learn that most of them practiced until they mastered the ability. Many speakers have to get in front of an audience multiple times (more than 25) to become confident, and they also have to know their subject matter. An effective speaker practices what he or she will say before presenting, and only after presenting many times can he or she give an impromptu speech about a topic. Once the speaker has mastered the subject matter and the contents of the speech, it will flow without further practice.

I found I had a different challenge. What was missing was my ability to build adequate rapport with others. In the classroom, the teacher is automatically the authority. I established a special rapport based on the pre-established roles. In addition to the incident in elementary school, my father was a humble man and rarely exerted his influence among his peers. This added to my habit of often being quiet in groups and listening more that talking. When I spoke, I said little. I figured I would have a greater impact when I did express myself, but this turned out to be a false assumption because I also had to craft my message to be influential. What I also did not know was that, without rapport, no amount of attention from those I spoke to mattered.

What the ##!! Is Rapport?

Rapport can be defined as establishing common ground between yourself and someone else. Until you do that, others are not likely to listen to or be influenced by you. This is a fine art. Discover what you genuinely share: a place you both lived or visited, a team or organization you both support, where you went to college, the cars you drive, a hobby or some other mutual experience.

This element can seem to be inconsequential at first, but it becomes the bedrock for building the relationship. You will have a natural connection if you both have something in common. Beginning with the unifying element, you are able to bond. Have you ever met someone from a city you lived in before? You have common experiences you can talk about, something that others don't share, and this gives you an advantage for working with that person.

Once rapport is established, you can better communicate with your client, customer or anyone else. This technique is critical at networking events when you meet strangers. You want to ask enough questions and listen carefully to the answers to find common ground.

Note how a great speaker will pull you in with his or her first words. These people start with an icebreaker: a story, joke or personal experience that you as the audience can relate to and enjoy. Even if the incident is not pleasant, it is emotionally grabbing.

Authors must begin with strong hooks as well if they expect to get the reader's attention and keep it. Otherwise, the reader will put the book down and never read it. This initial contact with the reader is critical to creating the relationship since the writer cannot directly interact with the reader.

Once you create rapport, talking to strangers is easier. Conversation flows out of commonality, and, as long as you remember to create a dialog, not a monologue, to *offer* and not to sell, the interchange can proceed. An offer should not be made unless the other person indicates an interest in what you do. I never mind sharing what I do, but I tread lightly when talking about my services or products. I don't reveal my offerings until I am sure there is an interest, and even then I find it is better to talk generally unless asked for more. Unless I am directly prompted to talk about the offering, a follow-up conversation is a better time to pursue interest.

Since I help authors write and publish books, after establishing rapport, I begin of the conversation by first asking the person if he or she is a writer. Many people have ideas for the books they want to write and are delighted to talk about their ideas. I set a time for a phone call or one-on-one meeting if the person indicates he or she could use my help. Until that scheduled meeting, I consider what we are talking about as casual conversation.

Creating rapport is essential in communicating your brand.

For a deeper dive into impact see Appendix IV.

SUMMARY

Perception, language and impact all influence each other in your life and in building your personal brand.

How you perceive your world will mold your language.

Language can change your perceptions.

Knowing the best words and phrasing to elicit the correct responses is critical in becoming influential.

Many are impacted by the right language and have an advertising jingle or song run around in their heads.

Perception can influence impact because you choose your actions to convince others based on how you perceive them.

Your impact also changes how you perceive them.

PART III

ACTIVATE YOUR AUTHENTICITY

All other swindlers upon earth are nothing compared to self-swindlers.
>—*Charles Dickens, Great Expectations*

The privilege of a lifetime is to become who you truly are.
>—*C.G. Jung*

It is now time to activate your authenticity and understand how your personal brand works. This part of the book goes into depth about the facets of your authenticity. It delves into psychology and how people interact. These concepts are germane to building authentically.

Chapter 8

The Matrix

To activate your brand through your authenticity, it is helpful to fill in the Depth Matrix. How deep is your understanding of how you interact with others in terms of your brand? Consider the following characteristics: Depth of personality, empathy and presentation. Then, view these in the context of expression, value and persuasion.

PERSONALITY, EMPATHY, PRESENTATION

DEPTH OF PERSONALITY

Depth of personality refers to how authentic an impression you make. Some people are born charismatic, but, if you were not, you can develop a magnetism that will assist your brand. To impress, you need to lend energy to your presence. If you are just going through the motions of what you are doing, you will not be seen or heard. Reach into your passion for what you are doing and allow it to blossom when you are in public.

Many writers and artists as well as others prefer to remain out of sight while doing their work. Whether in a cubbyhole pounding on a keyboard, behind a camera or in front of an easel, without a strong brand and effective marketing, it is doubtful you will be successful selling your masterpieces. I was not naturally extroverted but, during a shared show with a visual artist, I got my wakeup call. A talented illustrator and I created a series of original prints with his graphics matched to my poems for our opening at Zachs in Denver, Colorado. We planned a grand event. We invited a band to play music throughout. At the halfway point, they backed me as I walked around the restaurant, pushing myself to read the poems in front each piece. Afterwards, I mingled, and people kept asking me where the artist was. He chose to remain out of sight, and I later found him crouched in a quiet corner until the event was over.

I realized then that if I were going to have any success, I needed to push myself to be *out there*. I later understood that not only did I have to be visible, I needed to do so in the way I wanted people to see me, i.e., as my personal brand.

Many speakers and entrepreneurs, on the other hand, are natural performers, so filling their brand with their presence is easier. However, even some speakers I know are only comfortable *in their brand* when they are on stage. The audience expects them to continue with their personas after they leave the podium and socialize.

Others also need to demonstrate personalities to be memorable. Whether you are a business owner, working in a company or leading an organization, your personal brand can open opportunities for you. One thing people who advance in companies have in common is that they are known. I often wondered why certain people were promoted and others were not. In almost all cases, those who moved up the ladder exhibited strong personalities (whether others liked it or not).

One of the skills I've learned is how to make a successful presentation. Public speaking adds to your depth of personality because you can articulate what your brand stands for and who you are.

DEPTH OF EMPATHY

Depth of Empathy is your ability to relate to those with whom you associate: your audience, readers, clients and others. How well do you understand the people who use your services and products? Do you have different ways to explain yourself and your products and services to them? A strong brand does not change even if the presentation does. Your brand should include more than one aspect of yourself so that you are able to tailor the part of it you decide to present. To do this, you need to know your audience. Authors identify them for a book, speakers discern them when picking venues for presentations, and effective business people research the needs of their prospects and clients.

To improve the depth of empathy, I use a three-*stop* process: (1) *Stop* talking and listen, (2) *stop* telling and start asking questions, and (3) *stop* assuming you know what they want and probe. Begin thinking from their point of view.

Each of you is excited about what you can do to help others and thereby support yourselves. When you communicate, your first inclination is to explain all about yourself. Whenever there is an extended pause in conversation, people are quick to rush in to fill it. You want the other person to know how competent you are and what you can do to help even though you may not know what they need. Unsuccessful salespeople with this tendency trip over their own feet. They are in such a hurry to tell about their product or service they do not establish whether there is a need for it, and, even if there is, they may lose the sale by continuing to press the potential buyer until they talk the prospect out of buying.

We have a listening crisis in the 21st century, and it is exacerbated by our ability to broadcast our daily lives so easily with social media. Courses in listening should be required before graduation from high school. Teaching and learning this skill can be one of the most important things to bring about civil dialogue. Students might also increase the ability to understand differing opinions and to find common points in order to move toward compromise. Without these fundamental changes, none of us will be truly able to hear each other and appreciate each other's brands.

The process of asking questions is another skill you do not learn in school but need to master. By asking questions, you can discern what others think and what their desires and needs are. The art of inquiry is one that can be cultivated. Asking begins with a genuine interest in others. This caring is the foundation of empathy. When you lead with a question, you show others that you are interested in them. What each of us likes to talk about most is ourselves—this is a constant. In today's world, many people believe that they are not heard. This is most disconcerting when it comes to family and friends. The reason is not necessarily that others don't care but they may be so busy and caught up in their own thoughts and projects that they are distracted.

Being a good listener gets the attention of those with whom you are conversing, especially when you ask questions that prompt a deeper understanding of what has been said. I have had experiences where I mostly listened, and afterwards the other person remarked how interesting he or she thought I was. That amused me, but I understood. If I do only 10 percent of the talking and I speak with the intent of offering value, others will remember what I say if I carefully craft my message. I can also shape my message based on what they say, leaving me free to listen instead of rehearsing my next sentence.

Finally, we all have a tendency to assume we know what we may not. Malcolm Gladwell termed this *thin slicing* in his book *Blink*. Basically, what he describes is a mental process we use to take a small amount of information and generalize the meaning to the whole. This may account for our shortcuts in listening where we hear a bit and stop listening because we believe we already know the rest of what is going to be said.

This non-listening technique can produce detrimental results, especially when we repeat questions, or, after hearing the beginning of the answer, assume we understand the rest.

Additionally, people are not always forthcoming in answering questions. The result may be that we think we know what the answer is but have not been given accurate information.

One more factor to consider is contained in the quote from Linguist and Semanticist S.I. Hiakawa: "I know that you think you know what I said but what you do not understand is what I said is not what I meant." Another way of phrasing this is that we each speak from a unique context constructed from our own experiences, upbringing, philosophy and other building blocks of our individual perspectives and forget that others have their own contexts.

Listening and understanding are not trivial activities or skills. To be a better author, speaker and person, each of us must work on them. Not only does this apply to actually hearing people but also being aware of how they perceive the essence and details of your brand.

Want your brand to be recognized in your communications? Shut up, speak less, and listen more. It pays off. When you are comfortable in your brand, you don't have to say as much about it. And then when you are asked, your crafted yet genuine, succinct message has greater power.

Since part of your brand will be presented digitally, how do you accomplish this task? You don't know who will see your webpage or your social media post, so this seems nearly impossible. Not so! Here are a few ways to approach the situation:

- You can present various parts of your brand on different pages of your website. Some use a variety of colors for the pages to identify the service or product.

- Email messages can be crafted for different segments of your list, so they will resonate with that aspect of your brand.

- You might use varied social media platforms to present different aspects of the brand.

- You can target diverse audiences with most social media platforms so that unique messages can be built with those people in mind.

One of my colleagues has specific background information for different pages of her website to reinforce the content on those pages. She is able to show a variety of services (and different facets of her brand) through each of these unique background images. The banner remains the same, but the background descriptions show the variety of her expertise. These shifts between pages subtly influence the reader.

Email is a challenge in marketing yourself today because of the glut of messages that ping your computer and phone. One wonderful benefit of email is that once you have broken down your list into separate groups, you can send messages based on the specific aspect of your brand only to those who would react to it. Numerous products also exist to build email lists with follow-up sequences and selected messages depending on responses you receive from members of your list.

Social media offers similar opportunities to target those contacts with whom you want to communicate and get immediate feedback. One of your offerings might appeal more to women who would frequent

Pinterest while another might be directed at those who like statistics and visuals and would prefer to see your information on Instagram. A business offering may be best presented on LinkedIn. Selected audiences can be targeted on Facebook and YouTube as well as other platforms.

In tangible form, a few of your options include:

- Create a variety of brochures.

- Have more than one spiel when you network or have a casual conversation with a prospect.

- Prepare a number of different fliers.

- Get more than one business card or use the back to promote a separate service or product.

One of my clients runs a fitness center. He has created trifolds for seniors, runners, bicyclists, weight loss participants, and those interested in group exercise. These brochures are printed on different colors of paper. People gravitate to whichever pamphlet interests them. This is the same concept seen in waiting rooms in doctor's offices with a variety of information available for patients to read and take with them.

The techniques are less important than understanding what facet of your brand you want to present and who your audience is and what you can offer them. With this in mind, you will be able to use your empathy to connect, and *connection is the key*.

DEPTH OF PRESENTATION

Depth of Presentation deals with how you show up in the world. I touched on this describing the image element of branding, but that is just the beginning. Presentation involves so much more than your appearance.

Another way to define your personal brand is how others perceive you. This is determined to a great degree by how you present yourself in person. This is not news to speakers; they spend a great deal of time working on the presentation of themselves and their materials, but, for authors and some of the rest of us who spend a majority of our time in an office or studio, this is not at the top of our minds.

Some people seem to be naturally distinctive, but many of them have crafted their images. Learning to speak well, select wardrobes, prepare elevator speeches, organize and plan for meetings—even casual ones—and to become comfortable in your personal brand are all skills that can be acquired with effort. Very few are born with all these pieces in place, but those with successful brands have committed the time to gather the missing parts and incorporate them into their brands.

EXPRESSION, VALUE, PERSUASION

Let us now explore the other dimension of the matrix: expression, value and persuasion. These concepts augment building a picture of your brand.

EXPRESSION

Expression is the ability to articulate your brand. How will you make others aware of your brand and keep that idea in the front of their minds? This is sometimes referred to as *stickiness* of a brand.

It takes somewhere between 7 and 17 touches for the product or service (and your brand) to become recognized. This need for repetition is why you hear and see the names of companies and their logos repeated multiple times in a television advertisement or hear it multiple times on the radio. To make an impression, you must express. I have listed many of the methods for expression already and will explore them in more depth.

To score highly in expression, you must use the most relevant platforms effectively. You can determine their relevancy by knowing where those you want to connect to hang out. What do they read? Where do they shop and what do they buy? What are their favorite online destinations? What blogs do they read? What are they searching for to gain information or solve their problems? Begin by answering these questions and initiate your plan of action to meet them where they are.

It is interesting to note that some people are so distinct and notable that their personal brands are inherently strong. You need only meet these people once or twice and the connection is established. These are rare situations, so most of us need to make an effort to put our personal brands in front of others often.

Your expression will be unique. By architecting your personal brand, you can devise a plan for optimal expression so that you stand out from others. You can differentiate yourself by crafting your words, so you do not have to one-up or be compared with the competition.

VALUE

Value is the next indicator in the matrix. Value refers to what is useful that you offer to others. If you can help someone by sharing knowledge that is relevant, you are creating value. By doing so you bridge the gap between what you can offer and what your client or customer needs or wants.

Determining what is valuable to your clients and customers requires the same research outlined under *Expression*. The most crucial questions are these: What are their pain points, and what keeps them up at night? Until you understand the answers to these questions, you cannot be sure you are sending the right message and providing products and services they will find worthwhile.

The value of your service or product may fluctuate based on clients' current needs and the economic environment. Keep promoting the value without pestering and you may be surprised how successful you can be.

I got to know Cedric through a few networking groups I attend. He sells a pain relief lotion. I must have heard him talk about the product 50 times and didn't think about it. Then one day recently I experienced pain in my elbow. Because I had heard him so many times, I contacted him and purchased the product, which works well for me. I have since recommended him and his product to a few people who also mentioned aches and pains. Only when the value was there did I reach out, but Cedric did a great job of letting me know what he does, and, when I needed his service, I hastened to contact him. Once I had used the product, I was willing to mention it to others.

A friend of mine says, "Always lead with value." I have learned that selling has to follow that value, and in my case I am willing to spend time talking with people about branding, writing and publishing—even if I don't see a possibility to work with them. The need may arise later, or they may know someone who could benefit from my knowledge. I usually gain self-knowledge in those conversations as well by learning more about what value I can offer or by expanding the number of people who know my personal brand and my passion for branding, writing and publishing.

Persuasion

Persuasion is your ability to create a following and build a tribe. Your personal brand only becomes powerful when others recognize, appreciate and promote it. You need to consider how you will encourage others to follow you and ask for your advice and help. Ask yourself why someone would want to know you or seek you out. What can your brand do to encourage communications and develop relationships?

These factors are represented in the Depth Matrix:

The Depth Matrix

		Depth Factors			Totals
		Personality	Empathy	Presentation	
Power	Express				
Factors	Value				
	Persuade				
TOTALS					

The rest of this chapter explains the intersecting cells for each of the combinations. When you have read through all the factors, answer the questions posed there. Let's begin by looking at the Personality Depth Factors.

Personality/Expression

You cannot express your brand without sharing something of your personality. After all, personal brands *are personal*. By revealing some of who you are, you can engage others. An effective brand increases the desire to know more about you and, as you share more, your audience wants more. Your followers want to be there for the ride and are interested in what you will do next. I have an old friend who is sedentary in his retirement except when he occasionally travels. When we talk, he asks what I'm doing now. He is fascinated that it's something new; he will continue with his routine and looks forward to his trips but is content to vicariously watch my adventures through my passions. I've gotten similar reactions from others and enjoy sharing what's new and watch their wonder and excitement for me with each fresh project.

I act similarly with people who interest me, and I make an effort to keep up with what they are doing either in person, via phone or on social media. The people I follow on social media are not necessarily rich and famous. What we have in common is that we keep moving and growing and share that growth with our fans.

Personality/Value

What is the value of your message? You want your brand to show itself as something of value to the general public or to the segment of the market you are addressing. Someone can have a *big personality* but little to share, and he or she may not have many followers. Even pseudo-celebrities who only share surface activities from their lives and/or gossip are providing value to those who crave that kind of information. It's easy to underestimate the *value* of trivia. How many Trivial Pursuit game nights have engaged and challenged people to compete with their knowledge? The value in these cases is entertainment. People do not live on distraction alone.

The value you offer should be congruent with your brand and aligned to your personality. I meet with a group of friends almost weekly, and I attend because each of them provides a special value. I can count on Steve to be cynical, expressing his world view with a dry sense of humor.

He peppers in some fascinating facts as well and is highly entertaining. This is his brand and he reinforces it by wearing somewhat outrageous Hawaiian shirts. Remy is always quick with a compliment and updates us on computer and high-tech news. Don is a business coach who discusses professional topics and is interested in RVs. Paul is an expert about eBay. Each of these people brings value to the meeting.

Personality/Persuasion

Your ability to influence others is dependent on your message and also on how people see you when you meet and communicate in person or interact remotely. As stated earlier, some people are born with charisma. They naturally command attention. Anyone, however, can have an impact on others. Each of you has a unique view of the world and can express your personality in interesting ways. Even the introvert can exert this influence although it may be in a smaller setting or in a quieter environment or through social media. Some of the most prolific online posters are not comfortable in face-to-face situations, but they have immense impact when sitting at the computer screen.

Richard, a writer whose blog I follow, spends a lot of time in quiet contemplation. He posts the most interesting short essays on Facebook and gets upwards of 100 responses. Since his writing is well thought out, the answers are normally penetrating as well. Watching or participating in his discussions is stimulating and often challenges the way I think about things. Richard is having a powerful influence on me and others via the web.

In the 21st century, the strength of the political wrangling on the web has increased. People post in an effort to influence others' perceptions on a myriad of issues. Some must believe that this persuasion is effective since the practice has not abated. Both political parties have seen how powerful social media has become.

Putting your personality out on the web or when speaking to others is critical to how persuasive you are. If others feel a connection to you, there is a strong possibility you can influence them. If you use your personality to promote your brand and they connect to the brand, you may have a fan! Relationship through a brand can be enduring and profitable for both parties. That is one reason social media is used so extensively. Linking up in person is even stronger; the bond is more substantial.

Empathy/Expression

To help your clients or audiences know and trust you, you need to convey your genuine care and concern for them. If you can reach out and let the other person know that you are interested in them personally and this is authentic, a significant relationship can be formed. When you feel what your audience/client is feeling and imagine what that might be like, you build a deeper connection with an emotional base.

When I find individuals who understand the challenges I face and can communicate that to me, I want to spend time with them in person or indirectly. Kristen Joy and Natalie Marie Collins offered an opportunity for writers to participate in a virtual session every Friday morning for months to work on our books together. This weekly appointment to get things done helped me to write this book because all the writers on the call had the same goal, and we encountered similar obstacles along the way. The first minutes of the weekly remote meeting were discussion. After that, we all wrote furiously, working to make our deadlines. We continued to communicate via a Facebook group between sessions, and, by the end of the sessions, many of us had built relationships with each other. We all care and are rooting for one another to finish our books and get them on the market.

We shared our experiences by expressing them during the hour or later in the virtual group. This empathetic expression by participants and leaders strengthened friendships and revealed a lot about each person's unique personal brand. When some of us met at a conference later, we felt we knew each other and had lively conversations as if we had been close friends for years.

Empathy/Value

Offering value depends on knowing what your clients need. Unless you learn and care about who you are working with, it will be difficult to provide lasting help. As soon as your client knows that you understand his or her situation, that person will be open to what you are offering.

When speaking of empathy in terms of value, the important thing is to develop the kind of relationship in which you are dedicated to your audience's or client's success. If they feel you are co-partnering in what is being created or developed rather than taking on the project as a consultant, the sense of empathy increases. Your client may want you to make independent decisions. Even if you need to convince them to do the project your way, in most cases valuing their opinions is beneficial.

When your offerings meet their needs, a greater empathy can grow. This is *your emotional investment* in the relationship. Each time you can help, your client will feel closer to you and your brand and will be willing to do more work with you. Even if you slip up on occasion with a client, when you have created empathy with them, they will develop empathy with you (unless they are not mentally balanced).

I had a computer crash and had to spend days reconfiguring and reloading my hard disk. I was working with Marie-Anne to get her book up on Kindle and had to do so from another computer which did not have all the files. I had access to most of those files but had to find them and move them onto the secondary system. When she learned of the difficulties, she was sympathetic and understanding, so, as the schedule slipped, we maintained a good working relationship. This happened in part because of the communication we had during a previous project and during the early efforts for this book. We published only a couple of days later than we had planned, and she was able to work around the delay. Empathy breeds empathy and this can be extremely helpful when unforeseen circumstances arise.

Empathy/Persuasion

Want to convince someone of something? One of the best ways is to show them that you understand their viewpoint. Remember I mentioned how few people feel as though they are listened to adequately. When someone is heard and understood, there is almost an obligation to *listen back*. One of the factors in poor communication is not getting critical feedback that allows the speaker and listener to know that the intended message was received. Remember, a good listener has a better chance to get his or her point across than someone who is intent on only being heard.

Understanding the other person also allows the listener to glean where to start to convince that person to act or change something. This is one of the reasons salespeople are taught to find the objections to the sale. If they can determine what the issue is (usually price and budget, don't need it, etc.), they can answer the objection. As you listen, you will hear a reason; if you can get to the underling rationale, you have a great chance to persuade. However, you will need to really understand the situation and feel for the person before you can expect any change of mind.

Presentation/Expression

Whether you are addressing a large convention or in a one-on-one conversation, speaking well has many components. A large part of success in this area comes from proper preparation. You will need to know:

- Your content
- Your audience
- Your goal
- Yourself

Mastering content comes from doing the necessary research about your offering whether it is a product, a service or your company. For a product, know what it does and, more importantly, how it benefits your audience. Being able to explain or demonstrate it is crucial and remember to begin simply. If someone wants more in-depth knowledge, they usually will ask. Be sure you are making it easy for them to understand. Knowing your brand enables you to talk about the product in a way that is consistent with your other messages. Services are more challenging to describe, so I often tell a story about how the service benefited a client along with a short description of what it accomplishes. Again, begin simply; you can always expand your explanation later. Describing your company should be easy unless you and/or your superiors have not delineated what is special about it. If you are the owner, you have probably built the necessary messaging about your company. Be sure that this is congruent with your personal brand!

By considering audience, you will know that what you say is the right material for the right people. Many people work to precisely define what they do so they can easily articulate it. However, is it not also true that different people can benefit from a different aspect of what you offer? When I meet seasoned authors or speakers, I might ask about their sales and marketing, whereas if the person is interested in writing a first book, I can offer advice on how to get started. Having just one message is limiting. I suggest you understand who your different audiences are, so you can tailor your conversation.

Present with the end in mind. Ultimately, you want to work with this person if he or she is a good match. Before you get to that point, however, you need to fulfill other needs for the client. Initially, you will probably want to establish a rapport, and this might be the focus of your first meeting, not that you would refuse to take an order if the client is ready to sign on the dotted line. You may need to convince more than one person before they employ your services. The more expensive your services and/or products, the more steps may be required, especially for the initial sale. After the first sale, you may be able to offer your services/ products with less persuasion.

The final cornerstone of presentation is the most important: self-knowledge. Content, audience and goals derive from it. This is closely tied to the essential meaning of authenticity. Confidence to present yourself depends on feeling comfortable in knowing who you are and how you fit into the world. This is also the lynchpin of your personal brand. Having a good understanding of yourself will prepare you to present yourself and your brand in a self-assured and impressionable way. The exercises in this section will continue your journey to self-knowledge.

Your presentation is a combination of factors. You express yourself multi-dimensionally:

- Speaking voice and tone
- Appearance (dress, posture, poise, style)
- Body language

- Digital presence
- Video and audio (podcasts and video)

Successful people have learned good speaking skills or have a spokesperson who expresses their message well. A good speaking presence is dependent on your physical voice and your selection of tone. Your voice also refers to how you phrase what you say, your selection words, the pace of your speech, the range of your voice and your variation within that range, and other factors too numerous to list in this book. If you are not comfortable with your speaking voice, there are resources such as Meetups, speaking and presentation classes and Toastmasters™.

How you dress is also critical to how you present. A friend of mine with whom I did some video work told me that showing up as a producer rather than a videographer would help me charge more for my services. As a videographer, I had dressed casually; as a producer I wore a tie and sometimes a suit. His advice was sage, and I am happy I took it.

Whenever I speak at an event, doing training at a college or for a company, I dress more formally than my audience. There are exceptions such as in a manufacturing plant where that attire may be dangerous. The point is to look like the authority that you are.

Be aware of how you stand and your posture. Are you presenting from across a desk or in front of a crowd at a podium? In any case your posture should match the location and circumstances as well as your brand. Many presenters who sell digital products have an informal brand to convey that a common man can do what he or she has done. They do videos in casual clothing; some even appear in T-shirts and jeans as part of their brand.

Body language and facial expressions are also important. Your audience reads visible signals that reveal additional information beyond what you are saying. Body language includes how you stand and the way you hold your neck, legs, arms and hands. Facial expressions expose the emotions behind the words.

In Julian Fast's classic, *Body Language*, written in 1970, he talks about how many aspects of the unconscious and one's culture are revealed in the way you hold your body. He describes how personal appearance and choice of clothing send messages as well. He also details genuine and not-so-genuine smiles and postures and reveals what it means when someone crosses arms and/or legs. All these signals, many unconscious, are messages. The book may give you some ideas about what your body language is communicating.

The television series *Lie to Me*, which ran from 2009-2011, was about a group of consultants who conducted difficult investigations and arrived at the truth by observing and reacting to what are called *micro expressions*. The methods used on the show were an adaptation of the work of Paul Ekman and Wallace Friesen, who wrote several books including *Unmasking the Face*. The book describes these micro expressions for six emotions: anger, disgust, fear, happiness, sadness and surprise. By observing the interviewee's micro expressions—short facial expressions less than 1/5 of a second—the consultants could determine whether the person was lying or telling the truth. Your audience is also aware of these brief expressions, although unconsciously, unless they have studied this science.

One of the best ways to observe your own speaking, appearance and body language is to have a video made of you presenting. Watch it without the sound to see your appearance and body language; then play it again and listen to it without watching.

Your digital presentations include the text on your website and visual elements of your digital presence. Both aspects of your production are important.

One way many of you can improve your communication is with your use of email. Remember that email is a reflection of your brand, so, next time before you hit "Send," re-read what you have written. A well thought through message can do wonders to promote your brand since a majority of emails are jotted down quickly, not reread and sent. This can create confusion or at worst may result in losing a client. Use email courteously.

Personal brands can get into perilous waters in social media unless the messages are crafted to align with the brand. Many people will be careful when sending from a business account but are less vigilant when using personal accounts. Although you may not think about it, your brand on Facebook, Instagram, LinkedIn and other platforms is also reflected on your personal pages. Guard your brand like gold on the internet because it is vulnerable, especially with the lax attitudes about social media postings.

Your visual platform—on your website, in pictures you post on social media, your logo, any brochures or fliers you create—needs to be in alignment with your brand. Big companies and more recently some of the rest of us pay attention to consistent colors and shapes, and the style of graphics. A product on the shelf will reflect the guidelines set up by the producing company. This is a wise practice to follow if you do not do so already.

The other dimension of your visual platform is video. The same guidelines should be applied with the production of these.

Presentation/Value

Consider how what you present adds value for your clients. Most of your brand elements will not add value. Your logo or tagline, company ethics or mission do not directly contribute to what you have to offer.

When those new to networking start, they will excitedly tell others why they should buy their product or service. This is putting the horse before the cart; your offering must meet a need, and, if you do not understand the need, you cannot offer real value. The networking tenet to "give before you receive" applies wherever you are presenting your brand, your company or yourself.

To offer value, your presentation—in messaging, elevator speech, and web content—should address your audience's wants and/or needs directly. When you have assured your prospect that you understand his or her pain, you will be able to offer something of value.

I recently had someone connect with me through LinkedIn. I accepted his invitation and within a day received a request to promote his book to my contacts. Since I did not know him, I declined and closed the connection. No matter what value he was promoting, he didn't consider my position. I cannot cooperate with people whose only agenda is to use me to promote a book or product I know nothing about. There is no value for me and I would need to make an effort to learn about the book and author, which he did not help me to do.

One cannot overestimate the importance of value when presenting your brand and offerings.

Presentation/Persuasion

Building a persuasive presentation for your brand and yourself results from putting all these elements together. After completing all the exercises, you will have most of the components you need. The alignment of purpose and passion and tangibles and intangibles and the results of other exercises, including your insights from the Depth Matrix, give you the pieces to architect your brand.

The advantages to having a strong brand presentation are that:

- You are able to anchor the knowledge.
- You are successfully aligned with your best self.
- You operate from a space of increased self-awareness.
- You can expect increased synchronicity in your life.
- You can use your brand to ignite a better, more successful business.
- You will experience accomplishments that create personal and community fulfillment.
- You live authenticity in your distinct and notable purpose.

EXERCISE 9 THE DEPTH MATRIX

Now enter a ranking in each of the nine intersecting cells of the matrix. Give a rating of 1-10 with 10 being the highest score. You might want to use a pencil or, if you get the workbook or have registered, you can run off a copy of the pdf for the Depth Matrix.

Use these questions to rank each combination. You may want to go back in the chapter to get the details about each of the cells.

The Depth Matrix

		Depth Factors			Totals
		Personality	Empathy	Presentation	
Power Factors	Express				
	Value				
	Persuade				
TOTALS					

QUESTIONS

Personality/Expression

Question: How much of your personality is reflected in your brand?

Personality/Value

Question: What degree of value does your personality bring to the table through your brand?

Personality/Persuasion

Question: How well have you leveraged your personality to influence others?

Empathy/Expression

Question: How strongly do others feel your empathy when interacting with your brand?

Empathy/Value

Question: How valued do your audience and clients, friends and family feel when dealing with you and your brand?

Empathy/Persuasion

Question: How convinced are others that you are authentic in your concern for them?

Presentation/Expression

Question: How well does your personal image and perspective come across when you present your brand?

Presentation/Value

Question: How effectively do you communicate your interest and understanding of others through your brand?

Presentation/Persuasion

How do people experience the authenticity and power of your brand?

Gwen's Answers

Personality/Expression

Question: How much of your personality is reflected in your brand?

My brand reflects my personality to a huge degree. The things I write are deeply connected to my own life, experiences, and history.

Personality/Value

Question: What degree of value does your personality bring to the table through your brand?

Readers and students have recognized my heart in what I write and teach, and they have let others know about my work because they feel a meaningful connection to me and what I do. I've been told by those I have trained that I am the reason people attend my events and that my innate joy and natural enthusiasm inspire and infuse them.

Personality/Persuasion

Question: How well have you leveraged your personality to influence others?

Using my personality to influence others has never been my goal. Nonetheless, I recognize that this has been part of my path. People have tended to follow my advice and trust that I have their best interests at heart. Without seeking to influence, by simply coming from a place of heart, openness, and inner truth, I'm told that I have inspired others.

Empathy/Expression

Question: How strongly do others feel your empathy when interacting with your brand?

Empathy is a major part of who I am. I cannot separate my brand from that essence of my being.

Empathy/Value

Question: How valued do your audience and clients, friends and family feel when dealing with you and your brand?

Countless clients, students, friends, and family members have expressed how much they appreciate me for my kindness and the way I interact with them. When she was about to move away, one of my former students sent me a four-page, hand-written letter detailing the many ways she valued me as a mentor, teacher, practitioner, and an inspiration for her life. I felt profound gratitude for such a powerful gesture of appreciation.

Empathy/Persuasion

Question: How convinced are others that you are authentic in your concern for them?

I'd say pretty close to 100 percent. I may have offended a person or two along the way, but for the most part I live according to my principles and do my best to honor everyone.

Presentation/Expression

Question: How well does your personal image and perspective come across when you present your brand?

I gave presentations every month for many years and continue to offer them regularly, so I have a pretty definite understanding of what it means to express my brand. I believe my brand communicates who I am, and I feel strongly that I am living that brand.

Presentation/Value

Question: How effectively do you communicate your interest in and understanding of others through your brand?

When I write fiction, I definitely have to understand my characters. The reason I can do that is that I have a keen interest in people and find their lives and experiences both interesting and meaningful. As I stood in line waiting for my take-out pizza a few days ago, I struck up a conversation with another woman who had ordered before me. We talked until her pizza came, and I learned about her son and even the reason she was getting pizza before heading to her church. This is my life. No one is a stranger to me unless I sense they aren't open. I do my best to find common ground and offer a welcoming ear to those I meet. Yes, perhaps I may use a snippet of conversation or a quality of someone in a novel someday, but that isn't my reason for being interested in others. I simply am. It would be close to impossible for me not to come across as interested.

Presentation/Persuasion

How do people experience the authenticity and power of your brand?

I believe it comes across in the words I write and in the art I create. When I hold events, attendees generally sense the sincerity with which I speak and often relate to the stories I tell. I share from the truth of my heart and soul, and there's nothing more powerful than doing that honestly and with a genuine desire to help others.

Now that you have answered the questions and entered your rating in each of the boxes in the matrix, look at the sums adding across to see how well you are able to:

1. Express the brand.

2. Evaluate the value of the brand.

3. Understand the persuasiveness of the brand.

Viewing the sums added down reveals the Depth of Personality, the Depth of Empathy and the Depth of Presentation for your brand.

After completing the exercise, review your rankings and see if you want to change any of your numbers. Consider whether you have a different perception of the depth matrix.

SUMMARY

The matrix measures depth of *personality*, *empathy* and *presentation*.

These factors are measured in terms of *expression, value* and *persuasion.*

Personality/Expression - An effective brand increases the desire to know about you and, as you share more, your audience wants more.

Personality/Value - You want your brand to show itself as something of value to the general public or to the segment of the market you are addressing.

Personality/Persuasion - Your ability to influence others is dependent on your message and on how people see you.

Empathy/Expression - To help your clients or audiences know and trust you, you need to convey your genuine care and concern for them.

Empathy/Value - To offer value you need to know what your clients need and you must learn and care about them to offer the right value.

Empathy/Persuasion - To convince someone, one of the best ways is to show them that you understand their viewpoint.

Presentation/Expression - Speaking well has many components: Knowing your content, your audience, your goal and yourself.

By considering audience, you will know that what you say is the right material for the right people.

Your presentation is a combination of factors: Speaking voice and tone, appearance, body language, digital presence and video and audio.

Presentation/Value - When you have assured your prospect that you understand his or her pain, you will be able to offer something of value.

Presentation/Persuasion - The alignment of purpose and passion and tangibles and intangibles give you the pieces to be persuasive about your brand.

Chapter 9

Brand Identity, Image and Intelligence

BRAND IDENTITY

Brand identity has many definitions:

- how your brand is viewed,

- the components of your brand,

- your promise to clients and customers.

But these are just parts of the puzzle. The essence of that identity is how you use the external manifestations (your outer purpose) to reflect your inner purpose. This book discussed these concepts in detail earlier, and here is why these are so critical to your brand's success and ultimately to yours as well.

When someone experiences you, directly or indirectly, they form an opinion about you. That first impression is what people think of when considering you and your business. Although it can be altered over time, it may be a difficult process. When your brand is strong and is cemented to your inner purpose, you will be remembered. I already discussed that it takes more than that first impression for rapport and the relationship to flourish, but setting the appropriate foundation goes a long way towards creating those connections.

Have you ever met someone whose words and presence, no matter what he or she says, does not aligned with something deeper you feel? The words do not match up with another part of the message whether it is posture, gestures, facial expressions, tone or something that you cannot necessarily define. You know, despite anything that is said or done, that something feels awry.

Often this is a disconnect between the outer expression and the inner purpose, or it might be that you are picking up on a false sense of authenticity. Is the smile forced or just a bit over the top? Does the person make promises that do not seem genuine? These are all symptoms of a disconnect between something on the outside and something else on the inside.

A true identity will be architected so that the expression is a direct reflection of the authentic person. An instant trust can blossom from this expression between both parties. You have all experienced meeting someone and being *on the same wavelength*. A deep-seated perception occurs where both can see through to the other's essence and feel grounded in the experience. Some of my most fruitful business alliances and profoundest friendships began this way.

When you begin to build your personal brand, you are working on the brand identity. As you come up with the concept, you have seeded the process. You will be flooded with images for your logo, ideas for taglines, colors that represent what you are building, images and messages. These emerge from what you know about your passions, purpose and talents.

Developing a personal brand can be an interactive process working with coaches, friends, copywriters, designers and others to flesh out the full brand identity. You share the inner purpose and goals with these people to get the pieces you need. As a branding coach, I take clients through a series of exercises and questions and ask again and again to be sure we are working at the essence of the personal brand. The original answers will point in the direction, but we dig deeper to find the innermost motivations for the brand.

A well-crafted personal brand provides you with more confidence based on the work you have done to build the brand.

BRAND IMAGE

Your personal brand image determines how others see you and your brand and relays the value you have to offer. You want to make an impression that is unforgettable. What do you want to leave in others' minds once they have left the room? You want an impressive mental image.

You think in pictures and scenes, and this is one of the reasons that movies can be so enjoyable. Many people build their own movies as they fall asleep or as they dream. This is a natural process, so the vision you leave with someone can resonate with them for a long time.

Your image is hard to define; it is a combination of things that leave an impression with those you meet. Like your brand identity, when your image is aligned with the inner and outer you, the effect will be powerful. You want to be recognized in a way that makes others want to be around you, work with you and form friendships. Notice the next time you are at a networking event which people draw others to them and which ones move around the room meeting people. Either of these activities can support a powerful brand image. Some folks make an impression because they are great listeners, others because, after listening, they offer valuable advice. Remember how important it is to be heard. This discipline alone can boost your brand image significantly.

One of the challenges is to understand how others perceive you; you can gather clues to this by paying attention to how people react to you. Check out their body language, tone, the words they use and authentic or counterfeit compliments. You are constantly receiving feedback and the more of this you can gather, the better you can understand how you are perceived.

BRAND INTELLIGENCE

This is the power of your brand. Every facet of your brand connects and supports the others to create your fully realized personal brand. The brand promotes your authentic value to the outside world. You are confident in your own authority and can share it smoothly and attract others. You have come to trust your own perceptions and are ready to share them.

To effectively apply your brand intelligence, you must research your client, audience or readers. Determine what they need to be successful with their clients. Consider your client's knowledge and expertise. A series of conversations can help you discover these concepts and, of course, you must ask and listen carefully and understand their responses. Note the answers so that you can craft how you present your brand to them in the most receptive way.

Let's look at an example to make this concept concrete. A writing client was having trouble continuing to write her novel, and she confided that she had been formulating a response to a personal situation instead of working on the chapter she had intended to write. She was passionate about the letter she was writing and shared her exuberance. I suggested that the incident and her reaction to it could be woven into the story by including it in the narrative for the main character's mother. As we discussed it, she saw how she could write about her experience and make it an incident happening to the mother character. Then, in the next scene, she could reveal how it affected the daughter. By listening for her passion, I was able to get her excited about returning to her writing with a twist that could impact the whole manuscript and add texture to the story.

In a mastermind group, each of the people commented about the question, "What matrix do you use to measure the fitness of your business?" The answers by each member reflected the intelligence of their brand as they shared what factors they used to gauge their businesses. Each answer was a reflection of their knowledge but also of their insights about the people in the session.

Now that you understand the principles necessary to build a personal brand, you are ready to go to the next part where you architect your personal brand.

SUMMARY

Brand identity has multiple facets: How your brand is viewed, the components of your brand and your promise to clients and customers.

The essence of your brand identity is how you use the external manifestations (your outer purpose) to reflect your inner purpose.

A true identity will be built so that the expression is a direct reflection of the authentic person.

Your brand image is hard to define; it is a combination of things that leave an impression with those you meet.

Your personal brand image determines how others see you and your brand and relays the value you have to offer.

Brand intelligence is the power of your brand. It is the result of every facet of your brand connecting and supporting the others to create your fully-realized personal brand.

PART IV

ARTICULATE YOUR PERSONAL BRAND

It is not in the stars to hold our destiny but in ourselves.
> —*William Shakespeare*

The only person you are destined to become is the person you decide to be.
> —*Ralph Waldo Emerson*

No one saves us but ourselves. No one can and no one may. We ourselves must walk the path.
> —*Gautama Buddha, Sayings of Buddha*

If you do not change direction, you may end up where you are heading
> —*Gautama Buddha*

The first set of exercises allowed you to build the foundation for your personal brand. In the Part IV exercises, you will discover what makes you and your brand powerfully unique. These exercises enable you to build your brand and begin to:

1. Find your Distinctiveness
2. Become Notable
3. Tap into your Authenticity

The original name of the program was *Your Essential DNA* and DNA referred to Distinctive, Notable and Authentic. This is where we began.

Chapter 10
The Early Exercises

PREVIOUS EXERCISES

You have already finished the preliminary exercises in Part I.

You will use your results to work with the rest of these exercises. You may want to return to your worksheets to remind yourself of the answers from these:

Exercise 1: Uncovering Young Passions

Exercise 2: Uncovering Adult Passions

Exercise 3: Collate Your Lists

Exercise 4: Write out your Bucket List

Exercise 5: Examine Values

Exercise 6: Inner Purpose

Each of these exercises enabled you to begin the definition of your brand. This information and the insights in the intervening chapters have prepared you to complete the process.

Chapter 11
Distinctiveness

Can you tell me in 25 words or less what distinguishes you and sets you apart from others in your field or endeavor? Most people think they know but when pressed for an answer have difficulty articulating what it is.

Typical answers including saying things like, "I offer great customer service" or "I provide the most widgets at the lowest price" or "I am the best provider of my service." Any of these answers is probably also true for your competitors as well if you think about it. Even being the lowest price may not last, as a new provider may offer to sell the same things for less tomorrow or the next day.

The more you consider it, the more challenging the question becomes. The reality is that there is not just one thing that makes you distinct, and that is the key. **A combination of factors make you distinctively *you*.** This exercise is designed to help you define that combination that cannot be duplicated, that no one can authentically copy.

What is distinct about you is tied up with what makes you notable and authentic but the easiest way to untangle this puzzle is to begin with your distinctiveness.

Distinctness is driven by your specific strengths, passions, purpose and more.

Passions

Passions are what you love. I discussed passions at length in Part I and you compiled your passion lists in the early exercises.

As you architect your *personal brand map* you will see what this unique combination of attributes is and how it anchors your brand. As you do this exercise, you will discover and record each of these as you define yourself. After sorting and working with these, your personal brand structure will emerge.

You will want to narrow down your focus to build your personal brand but begin with a wide view. To do so begin by taking the results of your Childhood vs. Adult Passion exercise and building on it.

Working from the list of passions, create four to six categories. These are the ones that are the most *important* to you, those that resonate the most for you.

Creating categories can be challenging. Here is how I do it:

1. Look at all the passions

2. Group any that are related.

3. Discover which have themes in common.

4. Revise categories until they are inclusive of your most vital characteristics

REFINE YOUR LIST

During one of our workshops, we had two people who wrote down that they had a passion to coach those in job transition. Both professed to want to help these job seekers. One was very skilled at helping job search candidates organize and manage interviews, track letter writing and create impressive resumes. The other taught people about appearance (what to wear, posture and body language) during interviews, how to ask the right questions and preparation for those interviews. They had the same passion, but diverse ways to express it. This difference began to reveal itself in their distinctive styles or personal brands.

Examples:

Our first example is Sam. Let's see how he works through his list.

Sam has listed 12 passions:

- Perfecting written materials for myself
- Helping authors create clear sentences
- Erasing clichés from others' writing
- Sharing stories
- Simplifying processes by explaining clearly
- Inspiring others
- Helping others pinpoint their businesses
- Kayaking
- Business and personal coaching
- Writing to excite
- Creating poems
- Softball

There are themes among these different passions. One can see that editing (both for his clients and himself) stands out and is expressed in a few diverse ways. He also has listed items related to coaching—business and personal coaching and helping others pinpoint their businesses. The next theme deals with speaking illustrated by telling stories and explaining processes. The final theme which emerges deals with writing.

A few other passions are outliers and may come into play later, but you can see that a majority of the passions fall into one of four categories and Sam is ready to define how the passions are connected to purpose.

Some of the items on Sam's list are activities that fulfill a purpose, others are more expressions of passions. The split between the two is not always easy to determine and rather than splitting hairs about which is which, understand that this confirms the purpose-passion connection you worked with in the early exercises.

Once the passion-purpose ideas and themes are culled out, the process continues with refining the four to six phrases that describe his essential core.

Sam has five themes which are:

1. Editing
2. Speaking
3. Coaching
4. Writing
5. Sports

Let's see another example.

GWEN'S ANSWER:

Here is an original list and the narrowing down to four passions:

Original	Narrowed to Four
Making art	Inspiring (Leading/Motivating)
Exercising	Creating (Making Art/Writing)
Writing	Designing (Refining)
Designing	Helping others
Helping others	
Analyzing	
Building	
Leading Groups	
Motivating	
Refining	

You can see that the process included finding passions that incorporated other interests and disregarding others altogether. The goal is to arrive at four passions that best define who you are today.

One of the challenges others who have completed this exercise found was that their passions overlapped. In the example above, note that some of the passion activities were combined and a more general entry was used, e.g., Inspiring (Leading/Motivating) and Creating (Making Art/ Writing).

Let's take the *Creating* category from Gwen's example. This includes both writing and doing art. She thinks about what elements are common in these two activities and delineates exactly what it is about each that she loves. Is it wordplay with writing or is it making up characters and imagining fictional worlds? While creating art, does she love the assembly of different parts to form the whole artistic piece or is it the final product? If it is writing wordplay and the assembly of the art piece, you understand that *synthesizing pieces* both in writing and art is the activity. If dreaming up fictional characters and building their worlds in writing and the final project in art, then the activity is *manifesting vision*.

EXERCISE 10
FINDING YOUR DISTINCTIVENESS

Begin with your passions. Take your list from exercises 1-3 and select the top four passions that most accurately define you. Find passions that are related and create larger categories. Narrowing down these items can be a challenge but is necessary. You cannot present all the depth of who you are at once in your personal brand; you need to create something that people can quickly understand and remember. To do so, select the four passions. Do not spend too much time; complete this part of the exercise in 15-45 minutes or less. Do not get stuck in analysis paralysis. Use your intuition and your intellect to choose. If the intellect seems to be taking over, stop and ask your gut which passions most clearly define you most of the time.

STEP *1*

Using this list, you will begin to build your visual personal brand through your *Essential DNA Profile*. When completed, this map will show you exactly what your brand is and will be used with other exercises to fill in the complete brand.

See your profile on the following page. You can get a pdf copy of this and the other exercise sheets by registering to get the complementary packet of pdf worksheets. As an alternative, you may order the workbook to accompany this book and keep your exercises together in one booklet.

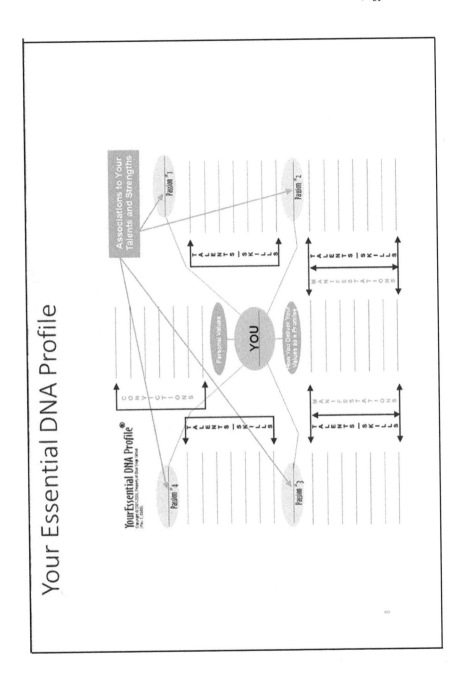

Write your name in the middle, then begin filling in the four passions above the lines for Passion 1 through Passion 4. The order of the passions does not matter. Put them in any of the lines in the gray ellipses.

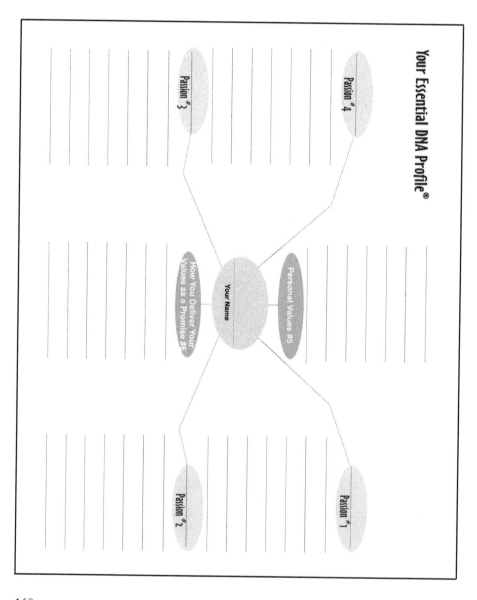

You have completed the first part of this exercise. Let's stop here and define some concepts.

Strengths, Abilities and Talents

Strengths comprise a number of the characteristics of distinctiveness. One of Webster's definitions for strength is an inherent asset. Another definition is "a good or beneficial quality or attribute of a person." However it is defined, you know your strengths are activities where you excel. There are many tests to determine your strengths including DISC Profile and Myers–Briggs Type Indicator. An interesting book that helped me define my strengths is *Strengthsfinder 2.0* by Tom Rath. Your strengths may be inherent, but they can also be developed.

Abilities are strengths that are inherent. You are born with certain abilities. Some people can naturally learn languages or paint or solve problems. Each of you is born with a different combination of abilities that you may or may not decide to develop. Whether you exploit the ability or not, it remains, although if neglected for a long time it may become "rusty" but can be revived. Think of riding a bike. Children learn to ride bikes but if they grow up and don't do this activity, they will need to begin riding again to hone their balance, steering and the other skills involved. However, one doesn't have to learn how to ride a bike again. Abilities are similar and if someone does not use an ability for a while, he or she will be able to use it after some practice.

Talents are natural abilities and must be practiced in order to master. One could have a talent to dance, but, if he or she does not pursue the activity, the talent is wasted. Think of Fred Astaire. He was born with the talent to dance, but only by dedicating himself the talent on a consistent basis did he become one of the best dancers ever.

Step 2

The next step is where the excitement growths. You will fill in six or seven activities that demonstrate how you manifest your passion. Write "ing" words to describe your strengths, abilities and talents for each of your passions.

Make discovering the activities for each of the four passions a fun and explorative activity. Take the time to reflect on yourself and how you approach the passions in your life. Allow yourself to focus on yourself; most of us find time for everyone else but not for self-focused activities. Gift yourself this opportunity because the results of this exercise and the following ones will help you better understand your life focus and empower you to share this powerful perception with others.

This activity in our workshops is broken into two parts, the first is to get a draft of the map and the second is to finalize it. Feel free to create more than one copy of the template or work in pencil so that you can erase. I suggest multiple versions, so you can go back because what you wrote in an earlier version may make sense later.

Whenever this becomes tedious, put it away and return to it later. Again, I want to stress that in the workshop we do these exercises in two parts on different days; many insights are the result of gestation during a night's rest.

NOTE: Do not let this become difficult and be sure to return to it between breaks as soon as you can. You may lose the initial energy if you take too long. I have included contact information at the end of the book. Feel free to email for advice Drew@RealizationPress.com if you get stuck. Please send as detailed a message as you can.

Personal Values

The next steps are easier. You will record Personal Values or convictions. These glue together your life. To discover which of them are crucial, ask three questions:

- How much of my life do I live this value?
- What do I take a stand for?
- What do I value?

STEP 3

List six and, if you are having trouble, take the opposition approach. Identify your values by asking yourself what bothers you. The actions that irk you are in conflict with your sensibilities, so think of the opposite and that is your value.

For example, if bullying is one of the activities that bothers you most, your values may be equity, perceiving the worth in all people, and standing up for the less fortunate. If those around you gossip behind others back and that gets your goat, then just treatment of others is a personal value. If instances of hatred and bigotry trouble you, love and respect are your personal values.

Most people can list their values quickly, but, if you are challenged, try the opposition approach discussed above. When you have completed this process, you are ready for the last list in this exercise.

STEP 4

Delivery

The last category to fill in your brand map deals with how you show up in the world. Write down how you deliver your values. This is a list of how you demonstrate your convictions. Another way to view this is to consider how people experience you and what they say about you. Contemplate what things people count on you to do.

Once you have completed your brand map you have 36-45 items that describe you. Realizing your personal brand is challenging because, as you see in your map, you are complex. So is everyone else. Now it is obvious why it is so difficult to describe your uniqueness in 25 words or less.

Examples:

Let's look at Sam Sample's Brand Map to see what a filled in map might look like.

Sam's map shows four passions: Writing, Editing, Coaching and Speaking. Each of these has been placed in a Passion ellipse on the map.

Your Essential DNA Map

Sam Sample

Personal Values #5
- Deep relationships
- Heart-centered living
- Cooperative working
- Empowering and Inspiring *
- Providing superior value
- Integrity
- Treating everyone with respect

How You Deliver Your Values as a Promise #6
- Collaborative Results *
- Deliver memorable writing
- Exceed expectations
- Open opportunities for further collaboration
- Deliver with quality on time
- Keep my word

Editing
Passion #1
- Knowledge of grammar
- Seek and destroy cliches
- Rewrite prosaic as crisp copy *
- Sharpen sensory content
- Encourage client writing process

Speaking
Passion #2
- Share deep emotional content *
- Provide value through my mistakes
- Provide short cuts when appropriate
- Inspire action
- Ask and answer questions

Writing
Passion #4
- Create poetic prose *
- Excite via brilliant images
- Convey information concisely
- Describe technical processes
- Create memorable phrases

Coaching
Passion #3
- Bring focus to your business
- Listen carefully
- Guide you to discover more about self *
- Ask penetrating questions
- Bring your personality out through products and services

His next task was to list his strengths and talents under each of these. Examining the fourth passion you can see that Sam likes to play with language (create poetic prose, excite with images and create memorable phrases). He has broken these down into each of the listings to focus on his delight with language. He also has added other strengths (convey information concisely and describe technical processes) which are not directly related. His listings took some work because he knew he had a passion for writing but couldn't put his finger on it. Once he spent time contemplating what it was about writing he really loved, he listed his strengths and talents. As described above, the untangling of strengths is not always a straight forward process.

After that he listed his values and how they showed up. Once the passions were finished these last two steps were accomplished quickly.

Now Let's View Gwen's Brand Map.

Your Essential DNA Profile®

Spiritual Wisdom Passion 1
strong spiritual connection
empathy/intuition
ease in meditating
love of learning
love of nature
connection to angels
studying/reading

Teaching Passion 3
listening/observing
communicating
inviting style
enthusiasm
knowledge/experience
storytelling
valuing students' uniqueness

honoring/caring for people, animals, the planet
peace
kindness
equality
living creatively
spirituality
honesty

Personal Values #5

Gwen *Your Name*

Writing Passion 4
listening
observing
imagining
outlining/planning
crafting/telling stories
poetic language
editing

Creating Passion 2
Envisioning
Divine inspiration
designing
playing with color
appreciating beauty
drawing ability
following through (on vision)

How You Deliver Your Values as a Promise #6
offering compassion and love
maintaining inner balance
being kind, courteous
treating others with respect
creative, inspiring writing & art
meditating/praying
being honest, keeping promises

Narrow the Focus

Once you have finished your map, take a break. Walk away from it for at least a few minutes and then come back and re-examine what you have composed. I was surprised how effectively I had defined myself, and I hope you are equally pleased with your work.

However, to craft a successful personal brand, you will need to have a final product that is easily identifiable so people recognize the essence of you and remember. Therefore, it is necessary to narrow the focus.

Many people resist this step and remark that the brand map is a good representation of who they are and to narrow it would leave parts of themselves out of the equation.

When I asked an author what she needed to do to be successful, her answer was *sell more books.* At first, that seems reasonable but what activities would achieve that end? The scope is too wide. As we talked she realized her goal was to *sell the next book.* That result was something she could work with by talking to others about that book, using social media, pre-selling the book and gathering a group of beta readers.

By narrowing the scope, she was able to define something she could set up tactics to achieve. The same is true of a personal brand: If your personal brand is a fantasy writer who has dragons and elves as characters, very few are going to be attracted to your pitch. A fantasy writer who reinvents the Knights of the Roundtable in 2045 with techno-wizards and ordinary people who can outwit all of them with basic intelligence might even raise some eyebrows.

Once you have narrowed the brand and can stand in your message, you will have a powerful presence to promote that brand. You will be able to live your life by design rather than by default.

Let's look outward into the world of branding. Nike made its name with a three-word slogan and a symbol (the swoosh) not even created by a professional designer. How did the famous three words "Just Do It" propel this company to the top of the heap? The slogan has nothing to do with shoes directly. It is about an attitude towards achievement that rang true for many people who aspired to become top athletes, executives or other professionals. The slogan was and is a strong inspirational statement filled with enough emotion to drive people to excel and get over all the excuses that may have blocked them. And it sells shoes like crazy. A great personal brand hints at what the person offers but inspires or entertains or touches an emotion and creates indelibility. This tagline was not an accident but the result of distilling what the company knew about its customers and taking a focused approach.

STEP 5

Selection

Back to the challenge: You have 40+ defining items on the page. To narrow the focus, the final part of this activity is to select six items from the map. You will choose from strengths and talents that define your passions, values and how you demonstrated those values.

Take one minute (and I mean 60 seconds) to do so. Select and mark those six items with asterisks. (You can see what Sam picked by returning to his Brand Map.)

Ready? Set? Go!

To focus, select the six items you have marked with asterisks and transfer them into the Your Essential DNA Code worksheet along with your four passions. It is highly unlikely anyone else would have the same DNA code as you. No one would have this exact combination of passions and skills, abilities and talents. Your essential DNA code is how each of you defines your own uniqueness. The answer to the question asked earlier (How are you distinct) is now a living, breathing document in front of you. This is a view of how you will fulfill your purpose as an extension of your passions.

You are about to build your Essential DNA Statement, which is designed for you to perceive your personal brand from the inside, i.e., from your perspective. This is not what you will share with the world but rather an anchor for you to use as you construct your brand.

EXERCISE 11 YOUR ESSENTIAL DNA CODE

Your final product here will be a short paragraph. It will be no longer than three sentences, but I have found that if you can compact it into one or two sentences, it is even more powerful. Being concise is extremely important here and honing each of your sentences is usually necessary. Your paragraph has to encapsulate the essence of strengths (talents and skills) you identified earlier.

Your wording may change to incorporate more than one strength or to explain it in terms of the whole of the six statements. Here are a few guidelines for your paragraphs:

- Write in the active voice.
- Make it compelling.
- Include how you see yourself.
- Consider how someone who knows you would describe your code.

One of the reasons for doing this part of the exercise is to view yourself from multiple perspectives. If you do not have a clear idea how others see you, ask. When working with clients who need clarification about this, I have suggested they email four or five friends and ask for a list of four words that describe them well. After compiling these lists, the client is surprised that many of his or her strengths are listed or words meaning the same thing appear in the replies.

Think of this as a kaleidoscope, one of those children's toys that fragments with the lens and shows multiple angles of what is being seen. Many views of the same objects give new perspectives and present different perceptions.

Refine your paragraph; look at each sentence and remove any filler words. It should be short and succinct. Your final version may take a few tries. Work on the statement until you are excited about it.

For the final step, to make this concrete let me share an example with you based on the strengths delineated previously.

Your Essential DNA CODE®

NAME: _____

Transfer your four passionate activities or processes

| Passion #1 | Passion #2 | Passion #3 | Passion #4 |

Transfer your six highlights of your four selected talents/skills, one personal value and one promise you deliver:

| Talent/Skill #1 | + | Talent/Skill #2 | + | Talent/Skill #3 |
| Talent/Skill #4 | + | Personal Value #5 | + | Promises You Deliver #6 |

Re-Order your six highlights so they tell a story:

| #___ | + | #___ | + | #___ |
| #___ | + | #___ | + | #___ |

Your Essential DNA Statement (Put the re-ordered six highlights into a sentence by adding a few connecting words and simple verbs, if necessary)

_____

_____

_____

Examples:

In the following example for **Sam's Essential DNA Code**, you see he has filled in all his passions, talents/skills and his value and delivery lines with his selections that had asterisks.

Your Essential DNA CODE — NAME: Sam Sample

Sam's Essential DNA Statement is two sentences and encompasses all the concepts from what he had filled in the Talent/Skills section. He has focused on his abilities and how he works with clients, so we see him through more than one perspective. In the first sentence, Sam reveals what he brings to his relationships with clients and in the second what goals and results he expects for them.

GWEN'S ESSENTIAL DNA STATEMENT:

Your Essential DNA CODE

NAME: Gwen

Transfer your four passionate activities or processes

Writing	Creating	Teaching	Spiritual Wisdom
Passion #1	Passion #2	Passion #3	Passion #4

Transfer your six highlights of your four selected talents/skills, one personal value and one promise you deliver:

crafting/telling stories **+** divine inspiration **+** communicating
Talent/Skill 1 — Talent/Skill 2 — Talent/Skill 3

stong divine connection **+** living creatively **+** creative, inspiring writing, art
Talent/Skill 4 — Personal Value #5 — Promises You Deliver #6

Your Essential DNA Statement (Put the re-ordered six highlights into a sentence by adding a few connecting words and simple verbs, if necessary)

I live creatively, crafting and communicating divinely-inspired stories, art, and poetry. I share
spiritual wisdom and hold the vision of a better world.

This is NOT only one way to write your Essential DNA Statement. Depending on your entries, yours might be different. *If yours is different, that is correct.* No two people are going to complete this exercise in the same way.

What to Do with Your Essential DNA Statement

Now that you have your Essential DNA Statement, you have architected the basis of your brand. Your statement is a vision of yourself which:

- Helps you stand with greater confidence in yourself and your brand,
- Strengthens the connection to your brand,
- Aligns with your essence and empowers you to resist the push and pull from outside forces,
- Aids you in removing the filters of family, school and others, and
- Readies you to articulate your brand to the world.

Your statement will operate in the background in your presentation of your personal brand and you will never state it. Remember how "Just Do It" for Nike implies many things about the viewer's competencies and dedication to athletic activities? The Essential DNA Statement acts similarly, and, as you create your website, materials, courses, speeches, introductions and other direct and indirect ways to experience your brand, these sentences will resonate in your mind.

SUMMARY

Most people think they know what distinguishes them but have difficulty articulating it.

A combination of factors makes you distinctively *you.*

As you create a *personal brand map,* you will see what this unique combination of attributes is and how it anchors your brand.

Working from the list of passions, create four to six categories.

There are themes among the different passions.

Some passions overlap.

You cannot present all the depth of who you are at once in your personal brand; you need to create something that people can quickly understand and remember. To do so, select the four most pertinent passions.

Strengths are activities where you excel.

Abilities are one type of strength that are inherent.

Talents are natural abilities and must be practiced in order to master them.

Your Personal Values or convictions glue together your life.

Your Essential DNA Statement has to encapsulate the essence of strengths (talents and skills) you identified earlier.

Chapter 12

Your Archetype

The universal aspect of each person's essence has been the subject of study throughout the last century and into this one. One of the leaders in the field was C. J. Jung who wrote and did extensive research about the collective unconscious or what he later termed the objective psyche. He found that universal principles crossed borders and countries. All of us respond to a number of what he termed *archetypes*. One way to think of these is as roles we all recognize. Thinking of movies, you can easily identify one of the major archetypes, *the hero*. Everyone understands this role.

According to Jung, archetypes are images and forms that emerge from a collective nature of thought and patterns from practically all over the earth and appear in myths and simultaneously are part of the individual's unconscious.

Carl Jung, who developed the idea of archetypes, had this to say about them:

"All the most powerful ideas in history go back to archetypes. This is particularly true of religious ideas, but the central concepts of science, philosophy, and ethics are no exception to this rule.

In their present form, they are variants of archetypal ideas, created by consciously applying and adapting these ideas to reality. For it is the function of consciousness not only to recognize and assimilate the external world through the gateway of the senses, but to translate into visible reality the world within us."[4]

In our modern culture, they play a significant role in advertising, especially in visual media such as television, magazines, billboards and other graphic forms, and crop up all around us. They are so pervasive you do not usually recognize them unless you are looking for them.

Archetypes help us to see how your audiences and clients see you. They also reveal your self-perception. By understanding which archetypes resonate with you, you have another measure of who you are. This knowledge is useful in building the personal brand.

You can understand which of these archetypes belong to your brand by taking the archetype quiz. We designed this exercise for the Purpose Powered Process workshop, and I have used it during presentations. Participant feedback has vetted the exercise. Your top three selections help to define you and your brand.

In the worksheet below, assign a value to each statement. Use the following guide as you rank each:

5	All the time
4	Most of the time
3	Sometimes
2	Rarely
1	Never

Do not assign more than five "5" values for this exercise.

	STATEMENTS	VALUE 0-5
1	I long for the simple, perfect life.	
2	I want freedom to find my authenticity.	
3	I think for myself, hold my own opinions, create my own models.	
4	I will find a way to accomplish the task.	
5	I question authority.	
6	I can transform the world.	
7	I believe everyone matters just as they are.	
8	I desire to be attractive and special to others.	
9	I enjoy being myself, allowing my playfulness to make the world lighter.	
10	I am here to help and nurture others.	
11	I desire to live self-expressively.	
12	I take leadership for the groups I am in.	
13	I think about the best systems to organize for efficiency & stability.	
14	I want to create and share my vision.	
15	I seek a balance in caring for myself and for others.	
16	I love making jokes; they point out the absurdities in life.	
17	I desire to have close friends and know each other well.	
18	I root for the underdog.	
19	I create to make dreams come true.	
20	I want to disrupt or destroy what doesn't work.	
21	I will make the world a better place.	
22	I want to share my expertise with others.	
23	I search for the new in the outside world to see how it might fit with my inner world.	
24	My work helps others to renew themselves through fundamental values.	

EXERCISE 12 WHICH ARCHETYPES ARE YOU?

Look through the statements and then assign your numbers. You may want to use a pencil because you may change your mind once or twice. Work quickly; dedicate a maximum of seven minutes to assigning the statements. You may use the figure on the next page or sign up for a pdf package.

Do not turn to the next page until you have completed putting the values in for all the statements.

	STATEMENTS	VALUE 0-5
1	I long for the simple, perfect life.	
2	I want freedom to find my authenticity.	
3	I think for myself, hold my own opinions, create my own models.	
4	I will find a way to accomplish the task.	
5	I question authority.	
6	I can transform the world.	
7	I believe everyone matters just as they are.	
8	I desire to be attractive and special to others.	
9	I enjoy being myself, allowing my playfulness to make the world lighter.	
10	I am here to help and nurture others.	
11	I desire to live self-expressively.	
12	I take leadership for the groups I am in.	
13	I think about the best systems to organize for efficiency & stability.	
14	I want to create and share my vision.	
15	I seek a balance in caring for myself and for others.	
16	I love making jokes; they point out the absurdities in life.	
17	I desire to have close friends and know each other well.	
18	I root for the underdog.	
19	I create to make dreams come true.	
20	I want to disrupt or destroy what doesn't work.	
21	I will make the world a better place.	
22	I want to share my expertise with others.	
23	I search for the new in the outside world to see how it might fit with my inner world.	
24	My work helps others to renew themselves through fundamental values.	

EVALUATION

Once you have completed the list, fill in the "Added Scores." You do this by adding items from the top and bottom, i.e., add values for 1 and 24 and put the total in the Added Score column for number 1.

Do the same for 2 and 23, 3 and 22, 4 and 21, 5 and 20, 6 and 19, 7 and 18, 8 and 17, 9 and 16, 10 and 15, 11 and 14, 12 and 13 writing the score in columns 2-12.

You may want to cross out item numbers to keep track. Once you have the scores in rows 1-12, select the top three. Many times our participants will have multiple high scores. Go back and re-read the statements that combined to make that total and compare with other Added Scores. Rank those that are ties so that you can determine your top three.

	Statement	Value	+ Score	Top 3
1	I long for the simple, perfect life.			
2	I want freedom to find my authenticity.			
3	I think for myself, hold my own opinions, create my own models.			
4	I will find a way to accomplish the task.			
5	I question authority.			
6	I can transform the world.			
7	I believe everyone matters just as they are.			
8	I desire to be attractive and special to others.			
9	I enjoy being myself, allowing my playfulness to make the world lighter.			
10	I am here to help and nurture others.			
11	I desire to live self-expressively.			
12	I take leadership for the groups I am in.			
13	I think about the best systems to organize for efficiency & stability.			
14	I want to create and share my vision.			
15	I seek a balance in caring for myself and for others.			
16	I love making jokes; they point out the absurdities in life.			
17	I desire to have close friends and know each other well.			
18	I root for the underdog.			
19	I create to make dreams come true.			
20	I want to disrupt or destroy what doesn't work.			
21	I will make the world a better place.			
22	I want to share my expertise with others.			
23	I search for the new in the outside world to see how it might fit with my inner world.			
24	My work helps others to renew themselves through fundamental values.			

THE 12 ARCHETYPES

Now you can discover what these archetypes are. Each of the twelve are described below with the associated number:

1. Utopianist

This archetype is attracted to certainty, cherishes positive ideas, hope, rescue and redemption. They are trusting and spiritual and have a utopian vision. They also are interested in health.

2. Seeker

Seekers seek self-sufficiency and a better world. They prefer wide open spaces and the night sky. These people are outsiders and ahead of their time. They yearn for excitement and appreciate authenticity.

3. Visionary

Visionaries are independent thinkers, researchers, teachers, and wise men/women. In *The Tipping Point*, Malcolm Gladwell referred to these people as mavens—those in the know. They are the early adopters of new trends and are interested in learning for its own sake. Some are elitist and will work only with the best. They value their freedom to keep an objective view.

4. Champion

Champions are disciplined, focused, decisive and inspire others. One or their main characteristics is that they do not see themselves as heroes. They are good motivators with a willingness to help, especially the downtrodden. They enjoy teaching others to be heroes and are constantly proving themselves.

5. Maverick

A maverick is an outsider, a rebel, a revolutionary and follows his or her own rules and values. This person wants to change how things are done and stands apart from main culture. He or she will often do what is considered unhealthy, uncultured and self-destructive. The maverick wants to return to the instinctual and has a disregard for propriety. A desire to shock and alienate are other characteristics.

6. Alchemist

The alchemist searches for and uses fundamental and universal laws. Other characteristics include a desire for personal transformation, the search for secrets of long life and power, and a passion to create prosperity. The alchemist wants to invent the new and create rituals. They are often entrepreneurs and strive to create their own lives.

7. Average Joe/Jill

The Average Joe/Jill wants to be part of the tribe, to quietly fit in and root for the underdog. He or she hates hype, is down-home, wholesome, frugal and genuine. These are the people who make life work. This person often uses self-deprecating humor.

8. Attracter

The Attracter is a romantic, values close friendships, seeks specialness and a deep connection with others. Other characteristics are appreciation of others and a desire to look beautiful/handsome. They thrive on shared likes and dislikes. These people are sensual and sexual with an aesthetic sensibility; they enjoy elegance and indulgence.

9 Trickster

The Trickster comes out to play. They are humorous; they seek fun and like to joke about serious subjects. These people break rules they consider stupid, dislike those who are overly serious, are truth tellers who live in present and do not mind looking ridiculous.

10 Healer

The healer is altruistic, compassionate and generous. He or she is home-oriented, interested in healing and may practice some form of healing arts. The person spends time on his or her own healing and worries about others.

11 Artist

The Artist could be a visual artist, a writer, or an innovator. These people are non-conformists, self-expressive and need to express artistic control. The desire for freedom and to create new objects and structures are additional characteristics.

12 Maker

The Maker wants to be in control and avoid chaos. He or she is concerned with image, with status and prestige and understands that how things look influence power. This type of person likes hierarchies, clearly defined roles and stability. The Maker is not only self-serving but wants to keep others safe and has a desire to help the world become a better place.

GWEN'S ARCHETYPE WORKSHEET:

	Statement	Value	+ Score	Top 3
1	I long for the simple, perfect life.	3	8	
2	I want freedom to find my authenticity.	5	9	
3	I think for myself, hold my own opinions, create my own models.	5	10	3
4	I will find a way to accomplish the task.	5	10	2
5	I question authority.	3	4	
6	I can transform the world.	5	10	
7	I believe everyone matters just as they are.	5	10	
8	I desire to be attractive and special to others.	2	7	
9	I enjoy being myself, allowing my playfulness to make the world lighter.	4	7	
10	I am here to help and nurture others.	4	9	
11	I desire to live self-expressively.	5	10	1
12	I take leadership for the groups I am in.	5	8	
13	I think about the best systems to organize for efficiency & stability.	3		
14	I want to create and share my vision.	5		
15	I seek a balance in caring for myself and for others.	5		
16	I love making jokes; they point out the absurdities in life.	3		
17	I desire to have close friends and know each other well.	5		
18	I root for the underdog.	5		
19	I create to make dreams come true.	5		
20	I want to disrupt or destroy what doesn't work.	1		
21	I will make the world a better place.	5		
22	I want to share my expertise with others.	5		
23	I search for the new in the outside world to see how it might fit with my inner world.	4		
24	My work helps others to renew themselves through fundamental values.	5		

Gwen's three archetypes are Artist, Champion and Visionary.

Using Your Archetype Information

With knowledge of your top three archetypes, your view of yourself is available from another perspective. When you discover what your top three archetypes are, you have a better idea of how to describe yourself and your offerings to the world. You also may find many in your audience or among your clients share an affinity for the same archetypes and will resonate with the messages you send them.

You can also identify your best clients and customers by targeting characteristics of those archetypes you consider your clients to be. You may have to do research to find out by building campaigns based on your best guesses of what will resonate for them.

For authors, your audience's archetype may be connected to the genre you write and should correspond to your avatar (target reader). Speakers will recognize that different audience members respond to different parts of your presentation. Knowing the most predominant archetype of your audience may help you craft your speech.

SUMMARY

All of us respond to *archetypes*, roles we all recognize.

Archetypes help us to see how your audiences and clients see you. They also reveal your self-perception.

Chapter 13

Your Destiny Statement

After working through the archetype exercise, you have completed your internal survey of your personal brand. The next step is to build the articulation of this brand. To do this, complete the I Am Statement. Start by answering these five questions. Each question is followed by an explanation, and you will want to use a separate piece of paper or the I AM questionnaire sheet in your pdf package.

EXERCISE 13 THE I AM/DESTINY QUESTIONNAIRE

BE AS HONEST AND DIRECT AS YOU CAN AS YOU ANSWER THESE QUESTIONS.

1. **When you think of the I AM, what is the first thought that comes into your head to finish that statement?**

When you speak to someone in a network setting or in casual conversation, how would you finish this sentence: "I am a _____."

Your client, reader, audience or prospect will form an opinion of you and your brand based on how you complete the statement. Instead of trying to form this entire perception, just write down any ideas and feelings that come to mind. You may also want to collect images. You might make a list or just write a series of words.

My example: I am a creative, an inspirer, a mentor.

I could spend more time and record more words and phrases, but this is a start. Notice that the words used to complete the statement are nouns that represent roles, not adjectives that describe emotions.

2. How do you naturally express yourself to the world?

The concept you want to share here is about your personality. We have spent some time discussing personality and expression to this point. Thinking back to the concepts introduced may help you capture the answer.

Are you an extrovert and outgoing, or are you introverted and stand back and observe before engaging others? Do you share your enthusiasm and smile, or are you more serious and wait to share until you are more comfortable with others? As an enthusiastic person, how do you encourage others to share that enthusiasm and reveal things about themselves? If you are quieter, how do you find your comfort level with others so you can share about yourself? It is possible for introverts to learn to share given the right circumstances. Although not the topic of this book, getting a better understanding of your personal brand makes it is easier to express more of yourself confidently without feeling awkward or worrying about oversharing.

What do you share through non-verbal communication and through your words?

My example: I used to be somewhat introverted (Remember, I lost my voice) but now enjoy talking about my entrepreneurial experiences, my books and publishing and learning about others' experiences. I have worked through my shyness and found a fuller life by sharing with others whenever I can. At the same time, I still treasure time alone and make an effort to plan and make that happen every day.

3. What are you genuinely dedicated to in your life?

Few people are reflective enough to ask about what is worth their life's dedication. In our everyday hurry, most of us take care of business and then at the end of the day enjoy family life or social activities. This works well for people for a while, but at some time (usually in their 40s if they have not considered it before) the question of the meaning of one's life emerges (the dreaded midlife crisis).

In what satisfying activities do you regularly spend time? What brings you joy? What has helped you create meaning in your life and connected you to the community/group/world in which you live? For some this might be your job, spending time with your family, reading for adventure or working on a particular hobby. In any case, write down those things to which you are dedicated.

My example: My dedication is to help others find creative outlets to live fuller lives and to challenge myself to continue creating.

4. How does your dedication to a purpose show up to help yourself or others?

Considering your dedication activity, how does it help you and other people on a daily basis? What benefits do you find from that dedication, and how do others benefit from your activities related to your dedication?

My example: I begin the day by writing a meditative poem and have done so for years. After that, no matter what happens, I have committed a creative act and the day has a positive beginning. This sets the tone for most days and initiates a joyful and grateful attitude. I look for creativity in those around me, and I encourage others to follow their imaginative nudges.

5. **What do you believe is the outcome of your dedication over an extended period of time?**

What are the results of your dedication over time? Consider what influence you have had on yourself and others because you have pursued this dedicated task. Can you record how some of these results appear both in yourself and in others? How do they make you feel?

My example: I have written over 1500 poems. Some I have read at poetry readings; some I have sent to others. I also have become a publisher to help others publish their cherished thoughts and stories and have taught many courses through various institutions. As a branding architect, I have also collaborated with others to discover their personal brands. I am proud of my achievements as well as those done by the people I have influenced, and my dedication has brought me joy and self-motivation when I reflect on it.

The answers to these questions along with all the previous exercises have prepared you to build your I AM Statement.

GWEN'S ANSWERS

1. I am a writer, a crafter of poetry and prose, an artist, editor, and teacher.

2. I began life as an extrovert but gradually became more introverted as a result of my experiences. However, as I've gotten older, I have learned to be more comfortable with expressing who I am and now definitely fall into the extrovert category. I still need a great deal of alone time, but I enjoy being around people too.

3. I am dedicated to expressing my creativity. Communing with nature and/or meditating feeds the storyteller in me. I spend time doing one or both to rebalance and feel inspired. Walking in the woods almost always beckons a poem from the ether. I love to daydream about potential books or the one I'm currently writing. Meditation often prompts works of art as well. I hope that my creative efforts in turn spark others to live vividly.

4. I feel centered, enthusiastic, and joyful after creating something. As a result, I'm putting out the energy of those feelings wherever I go, which has the potential to affect anyone with whom I come in contact. Beyond that, I've been told by countless clients and customers that my inspirational art helps to shift their energy, to get in touch with their spiritual aspects, and to view life from a higher perspective.

5. The intention of my artwork is to enlighten, inspire, uplift, and infuse with joy. While my fiction certainly seeks to entertain as well, there is always a deeper message that relates to making the world a better place in some way. My nonfiction is dedicated to healing and attaining a deeper sense of spiritual connection. All of my creative efforts offer the potential to rise beyond the stress and chaos of the external world and center in the inner truths that each of us holds in our hearts and souls.

EXERCISE 14 THE I AM/DESTINY STATEMENT

WHAT IS YOUR *I AM* STATEMENT?

Your I AM Statement is your declaration to the world of your personal brand. This statement is also referred to as the Destiny Statement because it points to where your personal brand will lead you both in your own life and in serving others including audiences, customers and clients, associates and partners and other businesses.

This statement is made up of three parts which are then blended together into one powerful statement. It is grounded in your *authenticity*, makes you *notable* (unforgettable) and is *distinct*. Your Destiny Statement is the culmination of your personal branding exercises and may or may not be used in its complete form to articulate your brand.

Answer questions beginning with your primary external goal and work inwardly. To do so begin with question three, then answer questions two and then one. This reverse order will make sense when you write your I AM statement.

Use your own paper or the pdf worksheet you have requested.

1. For the first question on the worksheet answer the question, "How do I serve the world?" We all can think of numerous ways that the world can be improved. Consider your vision for a better world. Feel free to use your imagination to visualize what your better world would be like. The mere contemplation of this idea and recording it will make it concrete and bind you to the service aspect of your statement.

Example: I promote creativity to change people's focus from themselves to a dynamic and peaceful world. If people are busy creating, they don't have time to be critical or derisive or unjust.

2. For the second question on the worksheet answer the question, "What am I meant to do?" In other words, what practices do I perform to accomplish the vision I just professed? Think about how you can make advances towards the improved world you envision. Deliberate about what activities, attitudes and daily routines can help bring this about.

Example: I mentor writers and encourage people to follow their passions and fashion something new, something never seen before. I know there's supposed to be nothing new under the sun, but I see projects on community funding sites every day that are new, and I meet writers who have their own take on numerous topics that have been produced before but not in the ways they present them. These innovators find new ways to present and new products to make.

3. For the final question on the worksheet answer the question, "Who am I?" Use information relevant to your archetype (but not the archetype itself because your goal is to be distinct), your Essential DNA Statement, and your passions along with all the other worksheets to fashion your answer. Many participants use a metaphor at this point and define themselves by comparing themselves to anything from an animal or natural phenomenon to a fictional character to their own version of a superhero.

The best way to discover your metaphor is to speak your answer aloud. Listen to yourself and if your sentence resonates with you, you have discovered it; otherwise, try again. If nothing comes, try completing the exercise with your guess and then go back and revise it. Your answer here may be a sentence or a phrase. Speaking this metaphor is an important part of owning it or finding that it is not yet refined enough for you to use.

My example: I see myself as a teacher/writer/inspirer—one with many interests and activities.

Gwen's Answers:

3. I seek to see a world where people live in cooperation and peace and in balance with the Earth and all life.

2. I write books that invite others to connect to the spiritual and poetry that evokes a love of nature. I create inspirational and angelic art that can energize or soothe, enliven or bring peace. The majority of my customers say the art has a profound effect on them. I plan to continue to create and publish such works in order to reach others and assist in the healing process.

I also teach classes that focus on healing as well as connecting with nature, angels, each other, animals, and more. I do my best to live as an example to students and clients.

I contribute to causes and charities that align with my values.

1. I continue to reach out to others at every opportunity, sparking joy and smiles from the heart. I laugh and play and reveal my creative side to anyone willing to listen and observe.

DESTINY "I AM" STATEMENT

3. What do you want for the world? What kind of world would you like to exist?

2. What are the specific actions you'd take and/or experiences you'd provide in order to contribute to what you want to see exist in the world?

1. What is the outward expression you authentically exude that gives insight into who you are in manifesting your contributions and devotions?

Drew Becker

My Destiny Statement:

DRAFT STATEMENT:

I AM _____

_____

_____

_____

FINAL STATEMENT:

I AM _____

_____

_____

_____

BUILDING YOUR FIRST DRAFT DESTINY STATEMENT

Begin by entering your I AM phrase from above, the answer to the *Who am I* question.

Follow that with your answer to the specific activities, your answer to *How will I improve the world*. A shortcut to responding to this question is to use the phrase *dedicated to* and follow that with the actions you take to accomplish your new world vision.

Finally, answer *What will my better world look like* and record your vision of that world. Describe what you see for the future based on who you are and what you will accomplish.

As you work you will see the elements of all three questions emerge in your statement. This statement can be revised at will until it is aligned with you, your goals and how you accomplish them. Remember that this also carries the power of your internal Essential DNA Statement without articulating it to others.

Draft Destiny Example: I am a multi-interest person dedicated to writing, mentoring and inspiring others to live in a more peaceful world.

BUILDING YOUR FINAL DESTINY STATEMENT

After saying this out load and getting a feel from it, then hone and revise it until your Destiny Statement resonates for you. Within a few iterations, you will approach your final Destiny Statement.

Final Destiny Examples:

My statement:

I am a Renaissance man who writes, mentors and inspires others to create or live a creative life to bring more harmony and joy into the world.

GWEN'S *I AM* STATEMENT:

I AM an artist of words and vision elegantly crafting poetry, prose, and designs to inspire healing, balance, creativity, and joy in service to the cause of harmony for and with all life.

Other Destiny/I AM Statements

Here are some other powerful statements by participants who have been through the program:

I am a lightning rod, grounding harmony, cooperation and oneness in the world one heart at a time.

I am an environmental magician, creating empowering physical spaces and trusting relationships.

I am a river guide connecting fellow travelers and pointing out islands of common ground so we can flow together into the sea of harmony with the natural world.

I am an innovator of new solutions to common problems and allow myself to believe that when I can manifest these insights, I will bring about a more abundant life for those around me.

I am a collaborator, an innovative thinker offering non-judgmental influence insuring a society where women are empowered to create their own legacies.

I am a catalytic healer for positive change dedicated to the process of self-healing to reveal my gifts to create a map for transformation.

I am a self-motivated trustworthy problem-solver helping others to achieve their goals through mentoring or performing services so that they can become successful.

Your Destiny Statement should send shivers up and down your spine since it is the articulation of your personal brand.

Please email me your Destiny Statement so I can share in your personal branding experience. Address it to Drew@RealizationPress.com, and I might use it in my next branding book.

USING YOUR DESTINY STATEMENT

Your "I AM" Destiny Statement is a declaration of who you are and does this by describing what is at the core of your uniqueness. You can utilize this statement to make choices or when you encounter a situation that demands you censor who you are or entices you to be someone other than your authentic self. You also can use it if you feel you are losing touch with your individuality and uniqueness.

How to Use Your Destiny Statement as a Compass

Good compasses always point in a specific direction (north). This does not mean that you always go in the direction they point. Nor do you always keep your eyes glued to a compass (that's a guaranteed way to run smack into trees). You use a compass to look at a goal or place on the horizon, then check it to see how the specific direction you are traveling relates to your goal. This gives you a bearing and informs you how close or far off your current path is from *your true north*. So, when you are faced with a choice or challenge, your compass is useful to discover quickly how aligned you are with your essential uniqueness and your destiny.

Anticipate Your Course.

Consider your life over the next few months. See if you can think of at least three specific situations coming in your future where you could use your essential compass to aid in making a major life decision.

Examples:

Should I expand my business to include mentoring people who are just starting to do the same thing I do?

Does this venue or group inviting me to speak align with my values?

Will this book agent promote my work to the publishers who align with my brand?

Should I co-write a book with another author?

SUMMARY

Your *I AM Statement* is your declaration to the world of your personal brand.

This statement is also referred to as *the Destiny Statement* because it points to where your personal brand will lead you both in your own life and in serving others.

Your *I AM/Destiny Statement* is a declaration of who you are and does this by describing what is at the core of your uniqueness.

You can utilize this statement to make choices or when you encounter a situation that demands you censor who you are or entices you to be someone other than your authentic self.

Chapter 14

Your Brand Expression

Now it's time to put your brand to work. You want your audience, prospects and/or clients to get a coherent view of who you are as an individual. People do business *with other people*, not with companies. This is the reason the *personal* in personal brand is important. To achieve a powerful personal brand, it must be articulated in alignment with who you are, your passions and your purpose. When these three factors line up, your presentation has the potential to impress others.

Here's why some people find this difficult: They have a split-personality brand. They present two different people, the professional and the personal. When conforming to a professional image or persona, their authenticity is diluted—the personal is muted or buried. In corporate life, I believed this was a necessary strategy, and I imagine others may feel the same way. Often those with a strong personal brand rise to the top with hard work. Their personal brand enables them to be *seen* in the noise that surrounds them. In a crowded marketplace, solo entrepreneurs, authors and speakers need to project a compelling personal brand to be visible and distinct.

To accomplish this articulation, you will have to understand three components of your brand. First, you will evaluate your business name or re-evaluate the name you have been using. Next you will investigate a tagline and finally describe the personality of your brand. In the process we will cover the tangibles (those aspects of your brand which people can experience) introduced in Chapter 7 when we examined the components of a personal brand. At this point you can work on the articulation of your brand, now that you understand what it is. Now you may understand why it is difficult to create marketing materials before the branding process is finished and why many companies have to rewrite and redesign them to match the brand.

THE BRAND NAME

Let's begin with the brand name. This is critical since the name is what your audience will first encounter. They may also learn about what you offer through the name. Others refer to you via your brand name, so it is how information about you is spread. With a successful name, others want to associate with you and remember you when they or someone else they know needs your services.

A powerful personal brand name has some if not all of these six interlocking elements:

- The name needs to convey **a clear meaning** that is significant for your audience. It will also imply capability and top quality. *EyeCare for You* lets you know immediately what the company does.

- Your name must be creative and imaginative for people to remember it. A lawyer I know renamed his law firm *Law++* instead of the typical partner named firm (Smith, Jones and Williams or something of that sort). The renamed firm sticks with a client or prospect because it begs the question, "plus what?"

If you favor creativity over clear meaning, your name may be less effective in print, but this choice can spark conversations in person. Consider *Horse and Buddy*, the name for an organization that helps people with special needs through equine-assisted therapies. Another example is *Damsel in Defense*. Although at first this might sound like a legal organization, this business actually trains women to protect themselves.

- A powerful brand name sounds good; it is **acoustically appealing**. A company called *Install-Rite* sounds like employees will do the work correctly from the start and, in fact, this is the brand promise they make and keep.

- The name should be **recognizable**. Most of us cannot spend the millions large corporations do on TV ads and magazines with massive repetition, but writers, speakers and business people can find ways to get their brands known. Recurring exposure through networking, articles, personal appearances and other means can make that happen.

- Successful names have **rhythm**. This adds to memorability. Listen to the rhythm in *Leapfrog Landcare, Empowered Ideas* and *Words Working*. Some of these names also have alliteration (similar sounds at the beginning of words).

- The brand name needs to have **emotional** associations. Brands like *Serenity Pet Massage* or *Connect to Clients* send an emotional message with their names.

A brand name that has all six is the most successful. However, some brands use the names of the person who owns/runs the company. For authors and speakers, this is often the case and once the name is known will work effectively. For those who have a product or service, a more creative name may serve better.

TANGIBLES

Let's return to tangibles, the expression of your personal brand.

It is common knowledge that you have to connect with your prospects numerous times before they will recognize you. The range I have seen is from seven to 17. You can reach out to people with tangible elements of your brand. The more ways you can get in front of your specific audience the better.

NOTE: Be aware that there is a saturation point, and, if you bombard your potential clients with messages and images, there is a diminishing return. How many of you have unsubscribed from a newsletter or email list because too many were sent? Not only do you not read them and resist following these messages, but you may avoid purchasing that brand. Think about it: Even television ads are usually spaced so you don't see them too many times and almost never in a row unless it is a mistake. Professional marketing and sales people know about this threshold.

Logo and Graphics

Logos and graphics are not in themselves tangible but appear on most of your branding materials, so they are crucial. Many people believe that their logo is their brand. The logo is certainly an important component and may be the first one many people encounter for your personal brand, but it is only one piece. This misconception about brands is easy to make since we live in a visual culture. As I have worked with clients, I have seen a handful of them design the logo first. Then, as we work through their brand, they realized their logo idea was not grounded in the full personal brand. They often had to revise or redesign the logo or have that done for them.

I want to include a note here about the importance of a professionally-designed logo. Finding a picture on the internet for your logo can lead to a number of difficulties. The image you select may be used by others and not be unique to your brand and business. If you or your designer do use an image, be sure you have the right to that image. Using someone else's material is illegal unless you make arrangements—usually paying for its use. You may need to get the rights to any image even if it is modified. Professional designers can help you navigate rights to the base image, then do modification, or can produce a completely new illustration for you. Be aware that any image—book cover, logo, etc.—that you get from a designer is their property. You have a right to use it but do not own it unless your contract explicitly transfers those rights to you.

Images such as photos or video you take are yours; however, you may have to get releases from people who appear in them or for certain locations. Please be careful to follow the rules about rights when building designs for your website and materials.

TAGLINE

Another easy identifier is a tagline. A tagline is a short sentence or phrase that is attached to your brand name. As a writing coach, I use "Get that book out of your head and onto the web or into print." My tagline explains what I do for my clients in less than 15 words, and I use it at networking events so that people remember me. An exercise to create your tagline is presented later in this chapter.

WEBSITE

Your website is the world's window into your personal brand for those who cannot meet you in person. Your presentation of your brand on the internet may be the only way some potential clients learn about you, so I am describing some of the elements necessary for a site to capture attention. I have discussed authenticity, distinctiveness and notability and these must shimmer on your site, especially your home page. People browsing the web will spend 60 seconds or less and only read one-fourth of the text unless they find great value immediately on the page[5]. Understanding this should motivate you to craft your message carefully and present it in an appealing way to keep prospects and clients on your page long enough to engage them.

Although this book is not about creating websites to promote your brand, consider having the following:

• Eye-catching graphics and/or video

• Text on your pages that capture attention

• Typography that engages but does not distract

• Something unique your competition does not have

• An offering to encourage visitors to engage

• Simple design

Living in a visual world, the graphics on your pages will attract your visitor's attention first. There is a tendency to move away from stock photos and find sites where photographers are offering their own, more natural pictures. Many websites include personal photos. However, you gather your images, be sure they are clear and crisp.

Video has become a standard on many websites. Consider creating or having video created and add that to your site. Connecting with clients via video can help build the rapport you need to attract and keep the ones you are seeking. The video does not have to be Hollywood movie-quality but should be professional.

Consider the text on your page. You need to pay attention to not only what the message is but also what fonts you are using and how many. Too many will distract your readers from your message, and too few may not present enough variety. Decide what message you are sending and be sure it is on your home page. Fascinate your visitors so they will want to see more. Reread the section on Message to remind you what needs to appear. Use larger, bolder type to emphasize what you want seen. Hiring a graphic designer who understands the principles of webpage layout is a good investment since they can build pages, so your visitors will focus on the most important content and their eyes will travel from one element to the next in the most engaging order.

Look at your competition's websites. What can you include on yours that they do not have. Is your video so entertaining that it presents you in a distinct manner? Does the copy (text) on your homepage provide answers to questions your visitors may not have considered yet but need to know? Do you have a graphic or infographics that are so memorable your audience will share it with a friend? Spend time thinking about what you can do that will help you stand out from others in your field.

Can you create a give-away that has enough value that your visitors will trade their email address to get it? This might be a newsletter, access to some training, a top ten list or other file they can download. Maybe it is a complimentary session with you or someone in your organization. Most people who are interested in what you are offering will share their email address, but only if they value what you are offering in trade.

Be sure to include your background and expertise to help people get to know you and why they would want to work with you. Include what is relevant to your brand. You might mention what you did in other companies, but the majority of this information should be about the brand you are promoting.

And remember to focus on their situation. This tactic works best on the home page and encourages them to look at other pages once you let them know you understand something about them and their concerns—this is the way to create rapport on the web.

EMAIL

Consider the signature on your email as well. The signature is the image and/or text that appears at the bottom of your emails. This is a perfect place to include brand elements. Whether it is your logo, contact information, your tagline or another message, including this in your emails is wise. Contact information gives the prospect the information they need when they want to contact you. If it is contained in your signature, they can go back to an email and get it. With smartphones, your number can appear as a link and they don't even need to dial, they can just click on it. Since you use email so frequently to contact others, why not take advantage of these opportunities to promote your brand?

SOCIAL MEDIA

Social media presence will probably be your most wide-reaching tool to promote your personal brand. Here are three steps to be sure you use social media effectively:

- First, determine which platforms you will use. This decision should be based on where your audience is. If you love Facebook but the people you want to contact use LinkedIn, change platforms. Do some research or test your messages on different platforms.

- Secondly, be personable but professional. Depending on the platform, there will be a certain formality or informality. Observe what others are posting and keep that in mind. Do share your personal style in an appropriate way.

- Thirdly, be consistent. Don't try to be on every platform because you may not be able to post enough on any one of them to make an impact. Better to post multiple times a week on one than once every two weeks on four or five.

Effective social media requires that you share some of yourself to promote your brand but be careful what you post. Offer enough so others appreciate you but not so much they ignore you.

There are blogs and posts I look forward to seeing. I follow a dozen people and read their articles on LinkedIn or on other sites. Some are professional, some humorous and others have ensnared me with their content. What all of them have in common is that it provides value in its own way.

Whatever you post from both your personal accounts and from your business accounts should be consistent with your brand. Remember this is your face to the online world.

Since the advent of social media applications—Facebook, LinkedIn, Instagram and other platforms—connecting with your audience is easier. Each of you can build a celebrity status simply by getting followers and feeding the platform with content.

However, this is a double-edged sword. I learned this in the early days of general adaptation of Facebook. In the early days of social media, an acquaintance with whom I connected posted about her gastric reactions to each meal she ate. This was intimate sharing but not something I wanted to read. I unfriended her to stop her posts but also avoided her at live functions because of the taste this left in my mouth. This was one of many too much information (TMI) posters I have had to unfriend over the years. Be careful what you post because it has a long shelf life.

COLLATERAL MATERIALS

Collateral materials are the printed pieces you use to share your brand. These range from business cards, fliers and promotional items to displays and vehicle wraps. You need to determine what will be the best way for you to promote your brand.

Business cards are still useful even in the digital age. You exchange these as an easy way to make a contact and leave something that can remind a new acquaintance of who you are. Spend time with a designer or on your own determining how you want this little card to represent you. You usually include your logo and contact information. How the card is laid out and the colors and fonts represent you so be sure these are congruent with your brand. You don't want a picture of a bull for a porcelain company (unless your brand is self-mocking and then this image may make it memorable). If you do not have graphic design skills, outsource this because it can make a big difference.

Be sure your fliers and posters are consistent with your brand. When you put on events, even if someone doesn't attend but sees the poster or flier, they have exposure to your logo and other branding components (color scheme, fonts, message, etc.). They are more likely to recognize your brand the next time they see another of your events.

Promotional items are a great way to make your brand more visible. These items usually include your logo and contact information and may stay on your prospect's desk for years. Pens are a good choice because everyone uses them on a daily basis, and, even if the brand is only seen for a split second, it registers. The same is true for note pads with your insignia on the side and/or on the sheets themselves. Unusual promotional items are often kept if they also serve a useful purpose. I received a full size padfolio over a decade ago and still use it. I am reminded of the brand daily.

Many authors and speakers have tabletop or floor standing displays for when they speak or do a book signing. Other authors like to distribute paper bookmarks or samples from their current or upcoming work. Be sure these include your branding elements.

The vehicle wrap transforms your car, SUV, truck or van into a rolling advertisement. Many people cannot resist reading what is beside or in front of them while stopped or driving and again you are making another impression.

PHONE

When answering the phone, a quick and clever phrase can help promote your brand. Most businesses answer calls by stating the name of the business, which is reinforcing the brand, but you can go a step further. When I worked for a coaching company called Inspire, we answered the phone by asking, "How can we inspire you today?" The additional phrase at the beginning set the tone for the conversation, and, even if the person calling had not considered coaching, posing the question could suggest the idea to him or her.

IMAGE (YOUR APPEARANCE + DRESS CODE)

The way you carry yourself and how you dress is another element of the brand. Remember what Howard Fast said about body language (in the Presentation/Expression section of The Matrix chapter). At a weekly networking event I attend, most of the realtors wear suits and ties or dresses. Loan processors and financial advisers don similar apparel. Web designers and graphic artists tend to come in more casual attire. Some participants wear polo shirts with their logos and others sport the same color ties week after week.

One colleague of mine shows up at events and in his workplace wearing a green shirt. Everyone knows that Alex will be wearing green, and this helps people identify him and is a visible part of his brand.

A speaker I know arrives in a bright red hat and a red blazer, and you can see her across the room as well as identify her distinct voice. She commands attention when she enters the room since she is loquacious as she arrives. As a speaker, she wears her brand boldly.

The ambassador for the town of Apex is always decked out in red, white and blue no matter the weather. JC sports a contagious smile and makes it a point to greet and shake hands with everyone. His presence cannot be ignored.

A few years ago, I purchased three brightly colored shirts—a deep blue, a brilliant green and a stunning aqua—and I am known for these shirts. I will on occasion wear a tie with them but more often do not. When I am in a photo that someone posts on social media or a website, the bright shirts stand out. I also have learned to try to greet as many people as I can at events and get into deeper one-on-ones with one to three people. If I cannot do that, I set appointments to meet them at a later date. This activity and my wardrobe have become a part of my personal brand.

YOUR TAGLINE

The second part of your brand articulation is your tagline. Taglines are used to make an impression that stays with others. It must be memorable. The tagline is a self-contained story and refers to the brand promise.

EXERCISE 15 CREATING A TAGLINE

Here is a four-step process to build your tagline:

1. Define what is important to your clients, prospects, audience. Write the tagline with words and in a tone which resonates with them. Be sure the audience will understand the words as they relate to your promise.
2. Make certain it is clear and advocates your strengths. An associate who provides services for business people at Reaching Higher, LLC uses *Social Media Marketing for Client Acquisition*.
3. Describe how your business naturally stands out from your competitors. This should be easy looking back at the previous exercises.
4. Build your tagline so it is easy to communicate. Ensure that it will roll off your tongue and that it can be easily recognized in print.

Here are a few of the taglines people I know from networking use:

*   Go4LessNow Travel – "My name is Judy, the queen of____" She pauses, and others fill in the blank by shouting "FUN!"
*   Words Working – Are your words working for you?
*   Systems of Change – Guiding Individuals and Organizations to New Pathways for Growth

- Team Nimbus – Helping people to realize their dreams is my goal.

Each of these fills the requirements for the four steps above. They are successful as far as being more or less memorable depending on who hears or reads them.

GWEN'S TAGLINE:

Illuminating words and art that inspire

BRAND PERSONALITY

The third part of your brand articulation is your brand personality. This is not your personality but your brand's personality. Let me explain the difference. It may seem subtle at first but, if you follow the example, I think you will understand. If you build the brand on your personality, you are telling people that your brand is you, whereas if you build it on the personality of the brand, you can expand and adapt it to your changing interests more easily. The best way to elaborate is to describe what happened to my company and why a brand personality saved it.

My original company was focused on marketing and used concepts that applied before even the infancy of social media for marketing. The company did business analysis, traditional branding, press releases and all types of writing for companies. When we added Misty, a video producer, if our brand had been built on my skill set alone, it would have been difficult to include the new skills we acquired as a videographer joined the company. Soon after that two things changed: I stopped doing traditional marketing, and I took classes in social media management. The company moved away from advertising and marketing and became involved in personal branding, video and social media.

Since the company was not attached to my name (but did have the underpinnings of my personal brand) a smooth transition was possible. Even when the focus changed to publishing (and I began using the DBA Realization Press), I again consulted my Destiny Statement compass to see that I was still offering services that aligned with my personal brand.

Had the company been named after me or built on my skills alone (like Becker Marketing), the brand would have been wedded to my offerings. By connecting the company values and hopes, the newly branded child company it spawned was aligned, and it was easy for me to transition the company and keep in touch with clients. They could still identify with Convey Ink but understood we also did publishing as Realization Press.

So, the personality of a brand is tied not to one person's presentation of that brand but to the Essential DNA Statement and the I AM Destiny Statement along with the other information gathered along the personal branding journey.

EXERCISE 16 BRAND PERSONALITY

Here are some questions to reflect on when considering your brand personality:

- How do you see your own personality? What type person are you and what do you think is good and bad about it?

- Is your personality appealing and empathetic? Does it help or hinder you with connecting to others?

- What is your brand personality, i.e., your intentions to serve others and your strengths to do that?

- How are the two similar and different? Where different, will this dilute the personal brand? If so, your brand personality may not be representative and may not be strong.

Separate your personality from the brand personality and build the brand on the latter.

GWEN'S ANSWERS:

1. How do you see your own personality? What type person are you and what do you think is good and bad about it?

I see myself as a creative, joyful person who loves life, nature, animals, people, and the planet. I can be overly self-critical at times, which in the past has kept me in a loop of rewriting and editing rather than completing manuscripts. Thankfully, I channel my perfectionism into my editing work now, so this is no longer a major problem. I also can be a little ungrounded, preferring to spend my time up in the clouds, which is the reason I need to spend time in nature.

2. Is your personality appealing and empathetic? Does it help or hinder you with connecting to others?

If you asked friends and family, I believe they would tell you that I am extremely empathetic (perhaps too much for my own good at times) and that I have an appealing personality. I do my best to be kind to friends and strangers alike. I definitely feel this helps me connect with others. I enjoy lifting people's moods wherever I go. Whether it's the checkout person at the supermarket or the fellow browser at the bookstore, I like to leave those I meet feeling a little brighter and better about themselves.

3. What is your brand personality, i.e., your intentions to serve others and your strengths to do that?

My intention is to uplift, inspire, entertain, and enlighten. My art is divinely inspired (often received through dreams or meditation). I've been told by numerous customers and clients that it enhances energy, joy, and spiritual connection. My work as a writer provides spiritual and healing insights as well. One of my strengths is following through on the vision. Another is the talent it takes to create art (both written and visual). My imagination and ability to visualize are key to the service I provide. As a longtime editor, I bring that to the table as well by making my writing as clear and easy to read as possible.

4. How are the two similar and different? Where different, will this dilute the personal brand? If so, your brand personality may not be representative and may not be strong.

Creativity and joy flourish both in my personality and in my brand. I feel the two are quite similar.

SUMMARY

People do business *with other people*, not with companies. This is the reason the *personal* in personal brand is important.

Your brand name is the connection your audience will first encounter.

Logos and graphics appear on most of your branding materials, so they are crucial.

Your tagline is another easy identifier.

Your website is the world's window into your personal brand for those who cannot meet you in person.

Your email signature is a perfect place to include a brand element.

Social media presence will probably be your most wide-reaching tool to promote your personal brand.

Collateral materials are the printed pieces you use to share your brand.

When answering the phone, a quick and clever phrase can help promote your brand.

The way you carry yourself and how you dress is another element of the brand.

If you build the brand on your personality, you are telling people that your brand is you, whereas if you build it on the personality of the brand, you can expand and adapt it to your changing interests more easily.

Chapter 15

Integration

In one of the workshops I was conducting with Sheyenne Kreamer for her group, a discussion about the concept of a personal brand's utility emerged. We had to answer the question, "What good is a personal brand if no one is buying?" We determined that utility had to be considered along with purpose and passion.

Soon after you feel the fire emanating from your new personal brand, you will want to integrate this new energy into your life and business. The discovery of your brand alone does not provide direction. If the process were to halt here, all your efforts might be in vain. If the passions you have discovered are unrelated to a job or profession, this might lead you to ask, "Okay, so now I know what I would love to do, but can I find people to pay me to do that?"

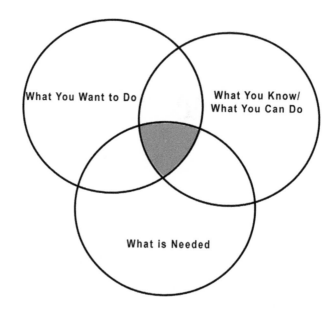

The diagram above demonstrates what you need in order to integrate your personal brand effectively.

Notice there are three intersecting circles. The one labeled *What you want to do* represents your passions and purpose, which you have defined in the first section of this book. The second, *What you know/ What you can do,* represents your skills, talents and natural abilities. It includes your knowledge and learned skills and what you are willing to learn to do. The third circle, *What is needed,* represents the current demands of the marketplace.

You already have an understanding of your passions and capabilities. Understanding the current marketplace cannot be sufficiently covered in this book. You have some of the answers already since you have been thinking about your customers or audience, but you may need to do more research to get a full picture. Here are a few suggestions to start that research.

EXERCISE 17 INTEGRATING YOUR RESULTS INTO LIFE

Check out those you want to work with and determine their needs. Answer these questions:

1. How big a demand is there for your products and/or services? Are other speakers covering these topics? Are there other books on the subject? Do other companies provide these offerings?

2. What niche would appreciate your products and/or service? Who wants to hear about the topics you speak about or desires the knowledge or other value from your books?

3. How many competitors are in that sector and how much of that sector do they service?

4. What are they offering? Even if others are servicing this market, you still may have something to contribute. Many speakers talk about motivation based on their personal stories, but each has a unique perspective, and those who are most successful share it enjoyably. If an author considers a topic and finds there are multiple books already on the market, that can mean there is interest and a new approach can be successful.

5. What can you offer that they are not? By searching the web, you can get a general idea of what your top competitors are offering.

Once you have determined that there is a need and it is not being satisfied by others or the market is not saturated, you are ready to proceed. With passion, your gifts and feasibility combined, your successful personal brand enables you to make a living doing what you want and are meant to do. You will need to concentrate on the wedge in the middle where all three overlap.

If you are missing even one of the three elements, your brand will be challenged. The following paragraphs describe the difficulties.

1. With passion and skills but no market, your efforts may be no more than a hobby since you will not be able to make a living doing it.

2. With passion and a ripe market but inadequate skills, you will not be ready to serve your audience or clients.

3. With skills and a market but no passion, you will have to march uphill facing boredom and encountering a lack of motivation.

You can have the desire (passion) and skills to make typewriters, but you will meet with limited success because there is such a small need for them. For the self-absorbed dancer who has honed his or her craft and invented a new form that no one likes, success also will be difficult. A book without an audience is never read and a presentation without interested listeners is soon forgotten, and the speaker will not be hired or asked for a return engagement.

I tried to take my personal branding program into corporations in the late '90s, but as a friend informed me, "It is too early, and they are not ready. Even if you educate them, there is little chance they will sign on since it is not mainstream yet." He was right, and I switched my marketing to solo entrepreneurs who were more open to the concept.

Many authors write books for themselves and speakers create programs, and, although they themselves are impassioned by the writing/creating and they may have mastered the skills, if the topic does not interest people, their works are unsuccessful. For other creators as well, if there is not an audience for your offering, it is unlikely to sell.

You can have the desire but lack the skills and even though there may be a need, chances are you will not be successful until you have gained competency. By that time the needs may have changed, or the market may be saturated. However, you may be able to enter the arena later and still be successful if the timing is right once the skills are acquired.

The third scenario, working without passion, describes how many people, who have just settled, live their lives. With passions buried or ignored, they do not see a means to enjoy the way they make a living. This is an all-too-frequent situation with those stuck in a job. They have *bitten the bullet* and keep going for an external reason. If they just maintain, just sustain, chances are they will remain unhappy unless their passions are revived as discussed in the beginning of the book.

SUMMARY

Utility has to be considered along with purpose and passion.

Check out those you want to work with and determine their needs.

CONCLUSION

You have taken quite a journey by participating in all these exercises and becoming familiar with the concepts behind personal branding from passion to purpose, perception, language and impact.

You have architected your Essential DNA Statement and your I AM/ Destiny Statement and can use them to fashion your messages from introductions to 30-second elevator speeches to website copy. You can use them in your social media to promote your brand by being sure that your posts, pictures, tweets, etc. align with your promise. (Your promise is contained in your Destiny Statement.)

To get comfortable with your personal brand, be sure to repeat your Destiny Statement aloud. Do this in front of a close friend or another person who has gone through these exercises.

For the next 30 days, please read both statements aloud once a day. It might be the first thing in the morning, at night before you go to bed or another time. I recommend you do it at the same time each day to make it a habit and easy to remember to do so. Take time to experience what it feels like to hear yourself say these words that express your brand.

Type both statements and attach them somewhere you will see them during the day. If you are in an office and do not want to share these with coworkers, tape your statements to your mirror at home or next to your computer screen. Take time to experience what it feels like to read it.

Feel free to tweak your statements as you work with them. You may find a better, more aligned wording as you do. Rewrite your statements and review your exercises for the next 30 days until you are delighted with your results.

After 30 days take the statements down. Put them in a drawer and begin to see yourself living them. You will find after 30 days you know them by heart.

Expect ripples. As you become more comfortable with your personal brand, you will find that the external world will reinforce it and your authenticity. Be grateful for these experiences, and you may want to journal about them. You may find that, piece by piece, phrases in the statements will resonate with you more and more and you will catch yourself living them.

Be patient and gentle with yourself. This self-examination can reveal insights you have not imagined. Allow your self-knowledge to unfold. Trust in the process. If you have questions or want to share experiences, please contact me. My contact information is at the end of the book.

Thank you for taking this journey. You are not alone. You have other readers and participants from the live and on-line workshops who have also been through this experience. Enjoy any insights and new perceptions you've had, and I wish you joy in following your personal brand to bring to you what you need.

It has been my pleasure to share this process with you that has changed my outlook, my business and my relationships.

I will write another book about personal brands and am looking for stories. If you have one, please email me at drew@RealizationPress.com.

If you benefited from this book, please leave me a review on Amazon or Barnes and Noble and feel free to contact me with questions.

All my best,

APPENDICES

Appendix I

From Passion-Purpose to P3

A BRIEF HISTORY OF PURPOSE POWERED PROCESS

I believe that an examination of how the program came about might be interesting for some readers. From its inception, the program has helped hundreds of people to become more successful through discovery of a strong foundation for participants. Let me take you through the history to glean what events led to the Purpose Powered Process (P3) programs and this book.

I first learned about personal branding when I met Genece Hamby in 2002. I was running my company Convey Ink, which helped clients with marketing and business branding. I attended every networking event I could find to meet more people and find leads for our services. At one of these events, a woman named Ellen, who had a company that made custom baked goods introduced me to a short, fiery redhead who was a bundle of energy. "Drew, this is Genece Hamby; you are both writers and might have some things in common."

We set an appointment for the following week. At our meeting, we discussed our life journeys as well as our writing experiences. In her recent employment, Genece had created brands for companies and products. She was talented at this and could usually examine her client's processes and products deeply enough to bring out the brand from conversations. She told me that these ideas seemed to jump out at her. She had enjoyed this work because of the constant challenge as well as the opportunity to continually use her creativity.

Her employment history was diverse. She had worked in a variety of businesses and had moved from place to place whenever it seemed advantageous. Genece had an adventurous spirit and followed it to create an interesting life. We bonded over the realization that both of us had desired and created unusual paths through our lives. We were also willing to carve out special niches for ourselves rather than follow the pack and we both enjoyed travel.

When Genece it a milestone, she decided that branding companies and products was not meaningful enough. She began a branding process, using herself to clarify the steps, and discovered the experience was profound. She intended to share it with others and was working on a new program she called *Personal Branding DNA*™. Genece had been working with her beta test group but invited me to invest in the opportunity to work with her. This 12-week one-on-one process took me though the most intensive personal investigation I had ever experienced. I had taken many self-development workshops by that time and had trained in healing arts, so self-discovery was not new to me. I worked through the process and dedicated myself to doing the fieldwork between sessions while continuing to market and produce for my own company.

By participating in the process myself, I understood what was missing for many of my clients: branding in their own authenticity.

When working with small companies, I found it critical to help them create an indelible impression for clients, and the best way to do that was to be authentic in their marketing efforts. Beginning with an authentic brand was the missing link. While going through my exercises, I was able to create the majority of the marketing materials I needed. By the time I had finished, I totally revised my website, my message and my intention for doing business. The concepts, as I interpreted them, became the foundation for my business, and I wondered how I could help others go through this process.

ARCHITECT CERTIFICATION

Synchronicity was at work. At about the same time, Genece created a certification program to train others to guide this remarkable adventure. I was among the first set of what were called *DNA Architects* to be certified. A dozen other people also participated, and we would work through the program and the underlying concepts in teleconferences on a weekly basis. We also did field work between meetings and studied the certification manual.

We all had opportunities to comment as we completed the training and thus helped tweak the course. I was consumed by the activity. Living in proximity to Genece, I could work closely. I got involved in editing the next version of the manual. We also had long discussions about several of the underlying concepts and enjoyed delving into the finer points of what she had envisioned.

The certification process ended with a written and oral test. After I completed these successfully, I took a client through the process with Genece. My wife was my guinea pig. Like most participants, she raced through some exercises and struggled with others. I was fortunate to see how she reacted throughout the weeks between sessions. I was reminded of my own struggles and procrastination with some of the work and gained insight into how someone else responded to the highs and lows of the process.

Working with Genece in these sessions, I also got a deeper understanding about how to present the materials. We continued to discuss the process with other certification participants.

MASTER CERTIFICATION AND BEYOND

Once again following her heart, Genece moved to San Francisco, California. She believed the next steps for her warranted a move to the West Coast. A few months after she relocated, Genece offered a Master Trainer Certification that would allow current architects to train others in the process. Four of us enrolled to do this work. The other three were in California. Again, I made a weekly commitment to Master Trainer Certification.

Our teleconferences went deeper into the underlying concepts, and our two to three-hour conversations often sparked new levels of richness for the program and furthered our understanding of how to train others to become architects. The certification was completed after I took a new architect through the process of training. Connie had completed the original 12-week program and then began her Architect Training with me. My practicum was to guide her through the 12-week process with a client of her own.

I had begun marketing the *Your Essential DNA Personal Branding* program through my company. I found it difficult to acquire clients because many who could afford the investment could not invest the time, and those who were fascinated by the idea and could make the time could not come up with the cash.

This dilemma frustrated me, but I continued marketing because I believed in the process. A friend of mine with whom I had done some branding work told me that I was just too far ahead of my time, so I refocused my efforts on a more educational approach for my marketing. Even this strategy did not yield the desired results. Another trainer I knew told me that it had taken her about three years to begin filling her courses and suggested I reset my expectations. Fortunately, during that time, I was also working with marketing clients and doing some writing and other training, which helped me to keep going.

In the summer of 2004, another Raleigh architect and I decided to build a live workshop. We proposed the idea to Genece; she was not enthusiastic about it. We, therefore, decided to build our course around design concepts and named it Life Design 101. We spent much of the summer creating exercises and building scripts around the concepts we had woven together. We beta-tested our one-day workshop. Most of our participants felt it had value but suggested that value was way below what we felt the workshop should cost. We advertised the workshop at a lower rate than we wanted in the fall but still could not get enough interest to run it.

SOUL'S COMPASS

During that time Genece developed a live workshop which she called *The Soul's Compass*. This two-day workshop was built from the first four or five weeks of the 12-week program. All the architects were invited to a few phone seminars to discuss *Soul's Compass*. The other local trainer and I joined the discussions.

Genece set up a presentation in San Francisco to introduce *Soul's Compass* to the community and recruit for the first class. I flew to California to join them in watching a pre-workshop seminar.

I met my fellow Master Trainer students. The marketing event gave participants a taste of the program with a couple of alternative exercises; it was attended by 35-40 people and, although it lasted a bit too long, the event was successful in recruiting a group for the first Soul's Compass weekend.

After I was back in Raleigh, I heard about the weekend workshop on a Master Trainer call. It had been wildly successful, and the interaction of the participants acting as "mini-architects" took the weekend beyond any expectations. Another workshop was planned for two months later in another city close to San Francisco.

I was in constant contact with Genece and the team in California. Their excitement was contagious, and the natural extension was an invitation for Genece to come to Raleigh to conduct the workshop here. The name of the 12-week program and the weekend workshop was changed to *Your Essential DNA*.

My Raleigh colleague and I marketed the course. I contacted everyone I had tried to get into the longer program and offered this workshop for about one-eighth the cost and a limited two-day commitment. By the time Genece arrived in Raleigh, we had recruited nearly all 18 of the participants who attended. Another architect, Bobby, flew in from Kansas City for the weekend, so we had a full complement of architects to help Genece with the participants. The Raleigh trainers worked out all the logistics, and the weekend turned out to be amazing. The energy in the room was phenomenal and almost everyone got into the process. What we had was an exciting success. Just like the San Francisco workshop, the interaction of participants with each other and with architects moved the energy to a whole new frequency.

Genece remained in Raleigh for a few months. A couple weeks after the course, I trained with her for a week to comprehend what was involved in presenting this program. We worked on each of the exercises presented in the workshop. My next assignment was to put together a class for October.

In the October class, I was the primary trainer and Genece was there to have my back. We had 14 participants, and another architect came down from Canada to help and observe. My wife, who had taken the 12-week program, was one of the participants.

Again, the workshop was riveting. One of the differences was that six of the 14 people involved in this workshop were male. That balance of energy brought a dimension we did not see in the previous presentation. During this workshop Genece confided to me that she had a new dream on the horizon that centered around art, especially poetry and perhaps something visual.

Genece remained in Raleigh for another two weeks to run an advanced workshop, *Articulating Your Essential DNA*. Ten participants attended that workshop, which was only offered that one time.

Genece went back to California and we continued to communicate. She started her new website, began digital painting and took time in solitude to write. In one of the conversations, she asked me if I would be interested in being the steward for the weekend workshop. We discussed this over a period of weeks, and finally we agreed I would take on the program so that she could concentrate on her art. She was contemplating a move to Santa Fe to be in an artist community where she felt she could flourish. I agreed to purchase the program from her and keep it alive. I did not have a full vision then but understood I had something extremely valuable. When I understood how to market it, I would be able to build something substantial.

Genece is now a pattern designer and has found her perfect job using her design passion. Her patterns appear on socks, scarves and furniture as well as other products.

I continued to market *Your Essential DNA* but got feedback that people did not understand the title or what the workshop included from its descriptions or its name. I began to work on re-branding the course.

I changed parts of the process to fit a slightly different perspective. As I substituted my stories for Genece's and revised activities, the program began to become mine. The name was changed to *Purpose Powered Processes (P3)*, which would include *Purpose Powered Person* and *Purpose Powered Professional*.

I ran a number of these workshops and, with the time needed for marketing the course, it was a full-time endeavor. The concept of a personal brand was still something new and finding people willing to try this was tough to be honest. Over the next few years, more people went through the P3 process in one of the programs. I also created an abbreviated version for community college programs for those in job transition and worked with additional participants.

Appendix II
Perception

How do you arrive at your perceptions of yourself and others? Perception is a complex idea, so let's look at a simple projection of it. Most people agree they are unique, but, if I ask them how they are unique, most give me a single characteristic (that they share with many others).

All of your communication and interaction (the vehicles used by personal branding) rest on the foundation of perception. Breaking down the components helps to understand how perception works. Since perception works through your conscious and unconscious perspectives, I will address the relationship between consciousness and confidence.

CONSCIOUSNESS AND CONFIDENCE

Have you been around people who don't engage you, don't inspire you or interest you? The reason might be that their own self-perception is negative and is projected in their communications. Even if you don't know why, you know there are other people you would rather see. These people might lack self-confidence or the ability to show it.

Those who believe they are so much better than anyone else can be obnoxious and condescending. They do not attract with their personal brands either. We all know someone who has to have the last word or who needs to be seen and over-talks or overacts in a room. People with these tendencies may be less successful in articulating their personal brands.

The optimal position is balance where one is neither overconfident nor underconfident.

The following table summarizes the relationship between self-consciousness and confidence:

SELF-CONSCIOUSNESS		
	Conscious	Unconscious
CONFIDENCE		
Confident	1	4
Over Confident	2	5
Under Confident	3	6

Those who have tendencies in the Conscious column have significant awareness of their confidence level. These people tend to have spent time and effort in self-understanding regardless of how they use this knowledge. Numbers one through six in the table are explained in the following material.

1. Conscious Confident

The Conscious Confident person creates a brand that is strong because he or she acts with a purpose. When activity springs from purpose, it is clear and precise. This is one of the reasons I covered purpose at the beginning of the book.

This confidence combined with self-awareness enables people to know what they can do and who they can help. In business, this fosters cooperation with others and co-ompetition (cooperation with competitors) with those in a similar niche.

Another characteristic of these people is that they have a plan and a way to implement it. This includes goals and may include dates. The plan can be altered but it needs to be used to create action. One of the more recent techniques to accomplish this is bullet journaling, which goes beyond a list and incorporates notes and scheduling. Since beginning my journaling, which I do mostly on my cell phone, I have created rituals that get me going in the morning and, by checking it a few times a day, keep me on task.

The next important concept these people use to stay aligned with their personal brand is living by design. This entails knowing what your brand promises and aligning your activities with that. Another advantage of a bullet journal is that you can categorize activities and quickly scan to see if they are moving you toward your goals. Living by design nourishes your brand.

Finally, conscious confident people naturally act in ways that *pull* others into action. They become leaders with whom others want to spend time and learn from to benefit their businesses and personal lives. As you can imagine, this is critical for speakers, especially motivational speakers, for authors who want to be seen as authorities, and for coaches and others who provide personal services.

2. Conscious Overconfident

Those who are aware and are overconfident can persuade but sooner or later may damage their relationships because they consider themselves better than their clients. The overconfidence can be a coping mechanism for those who are not actually confident and need to hide that. They may be sheep in wolves' clothing.

Overconfidence is characterized as over-aggressiveness. Because they see their skills and talents as valuable, they get an exaggerated sense of their own worth and underestimate others. This allows them to be aggressive and to force solutions on their clients.

Another characteristic is arrogance, which can parade as distain for other people or an unwillingness to account for their needs and input. This attitude is displayed by some salespersons, especially the shadow side of what used to be the image of the used car salesman. This person is so intent on selling the product or service that, even if successful, the buyer will not become a long-term customer or client, and the brand will have little sticking power. The next time the buyer is in the market, he or she will often look elsewhere where a relationship can be established. We have all encountered the pushy person at a networking event who is so intent on telling us about his great product or service that he or she never learns anything about us, even if we talk. These people are not good listeners because they doubt they can learn from anyone else.

The overconfident do not need a plan and live life reactively. They give no thought to what they want from the day or to their encounters other than to make an impression or a sale. This leads to a life in which, instead of action, the person is usually reacting to someone else even if they do not regard that person as important. They live by default and their brand is a brand by default. Since they do not plan, their brand is the sum of what others think it is. Without clear thought and planning, the brand is left to fend for itself.

Some of these folks can also be experienced as opportunistic, manipulative and bullying. They see every encounter as an opportunity to promote themselves and their products. I know an author who has sold many books because she is always selling whether the situation is right or not. Others are manipulative and will say whatever they need to in order to get you to act the way they want, to buy, or to sign up for some membership. In the past, a number of gyms used this technique to sell memberships until it was associated with the industry and people were wary to buy. Those who had authentic offerings in that business had to overcome this perception and show the real value to prospects.

Another example of overconfidence is bullying. We have become sensitive to bullying from children, but some adults are also bullies. This is usually demonstrated more subtly. One of my friends stop attending a networking group. When I asked her why, she told me about another member who badgered her so much to purchase a service that she preferred to stay away. Bullying in this manner is a powerful deterrent to forming relationships.

As you might expect, conscious overconfident people *push* others. The examples above demonstrate different types of pushing. We recognize this type of person and their manners, and, although they may be conscious of their brand, they do not understand how these behaviors harm it.

3. Conscious Underconfident

Those who are aware but not confident will act demurely and will defer to others when they may be able to add value. They feel that they are inferior to others, or they are shy and lack belief in their own abilities. This is a difficult situation because unless they take steps to gain the confidence, their chances of success in any field are diminished.

The victim role appeals to these folks, and they feel that the world is out to get them and that others create conditions that keep them from achieving. Playing the victim avoids taking responsibility for actions and allows these people to look outward for reasons they are unsuccessful.

Even with a plan, the underconfident may fail. They often engage in self-defeating behaviors because they do not expect to succeed. In cases where they do have a design for their life and brand, they may undermine it to remain in the victim state. One way to move beyond victimhood is to stop labeling oneself as "introverted" or "unable." Removing these labels from one's internal tapes and thoughts can go a long way in building confidence.

The underconfident folks are *pushed* by others because they do not have faith in their own ideas and opinions. When not anchored in one's own perspective and without confidence in the path to take, others' recommendations will sound like a better alternative. Self-development courses can help by increasing self-knowledge which can become the grounding necessary in one's life.

Those in the Unconscious column have limited awareness of their confidence level. This designation indicates that they have not currently expended the effort to delve into self-understanding. This lack of awareness limits their ability to create a powerful personal brand and be distinctive in their communications.

4. Unconscious Confident

Those who are confident but not conscious of why draw people to them but don't understand the reasons others feel that attraction.

Like the conscious confident, when they walk into the room, they entice attention and their brand is strong. These people see life as series of luck incidents, and, as a result they live by default. Since there was no acknowledgment of the self, the brand and actions are not planned and may wane over time if not cultivated. These people *pull* others into action.

5. Unconscious Overconfident

These people feel a sense of self-importance. They consider others less interesting. Their sense of confidence is not based in any abilities or accomplishments but instead on a sense that they are more deserving. They do not consider the reason they feel they are better than others.

Although these people may be good at what they do, they do not understand how their attitude affects others. These people are likely to miss signals from others and react only to their own needs and wants.

Coaches and consultants of this type are less effective because they do not listen carefully enough to work from their client's position. Instead they make recommendations based on their own previous experience. They fit the saying, "If your only tool is a hammer, every job is pounding nails."

Since these people are not self-aware, they do not have a plan but rather live by default. Having *all the answers* prevents them from expanding their experiences and thinking about what impression they might want to make; instead they move forward just like they always have. After all that's the way it's supposed to be.

These people will *push* others to action since they think they know better. They are not open to new options.

An overconfident unconscious person feels self-important and might be described as being born with a silver spoon in his mouth. He *knows* he is better than those around him for any number of reasons including status, money, moral superiority, attractive appearance, standing in the community, philosophical or political views or admiration from friends.

In themselves, none of these reasons is detrimental. In fact, some can be quite beneficial. The difficulty is the response to them.

These folks may be good at what they do but are unable to see their effects on others in the wake of their achievements. In addition, they may not see the need to recognize others who they perceive as *not matching up* to their level. They expect others to perform at their level and look down on those who don't. They are in denial that others might be equal or are better performers. They see others' activities as competitive and, therefore, are constantly making comparisons.

We see this stereotype as the religious person who falls from grace or as the great coach who turns out to be unethical or the marriage partner who gets caught cheating. They do not see the end coming because they are not conscious of people observing them. When confronted, they will blame others because they could never imagine themselves doing these things.

They live their lives by default since they have a history of riding the wave without thinking, introspection or reflection. There is no need to plan since moving through life has always been easy with no need to explore options outside of a narrow perspective.

Like conscious overconfidents, they *push* others to do what they want them to do. They may have many of the same characteristics, but their intent is less well defined, and they act without thinking about it.

6. Unconscious Underconfident

Those who are unconsciously underconfident do not know why they lack confidence. They have not done any work to understand why they don't feel good about themselves and have difficulty doing so because they do not feel deserving. They might say, "I don't know why I'm stuck," and they are challenged with where to begin to change the situation.

Like others who are unconscious, they live by default. They do not have a clue how they are viewed by others and feel intimidated by those who are confident or overconfident. They may wonder why others are comfortable in their skins while they are so uneasy.

They do not lead and are *pulled* by others into action. Without confidence and with no clear path how to get it, they are followers and rarely initiate unless forced to do so.

THE PERCEPTION FORMULA

I have gone far down this rabbit hole discussing consciousness and confidence and now will investigate in more detail the impact of perception on the personal brand. People who are unconscious are at a great disadvantage because a degree of self-awareness is important in developing an authentic brand. However, there are roads to move toward consciousness. To add to this understanding, I propose the following formula, containing the components of perception:

$$\underline{Con(A \times V) + UCon(Bs[P,Pj, I] U)}$$

Conscious perception can be described by the formula *Con(A x V)*.

Consciousness = Awareness   X   World View

Con is consciousness which is the result of awareness (A) filtered through world view (V). The consciousness is a product (in the mathematical sense) of your awareness of surroundings, filtered through (multiplier) your view of the world formed from your experience and what others have taught you. Combined, these factors create consciousness, half of the perception formula.

The other half consists of the unconscious factors:

$$UCon(Bs[P,Pj, I] \times U)$$

UnConsciousness =
(Blindspots [Prejudices Prejudgmets Imitation]   X   Unexamined)

These are the parts of your perspective you are not aware of. These are your *blindspots (Bs)* and include prejudices (P), pre-judgments-Look before you leap (Pj), imitated behaviors (I) magnified by unexamined (and in some cases unexaminable) beliefs (U).

Let's investigate it in detail. Once again the formula is:

$$Con(A \times V) + UCon(Bs[P,Pj, I] U):$$

Perception is the sum of your consciousness and the underlying aspects of your unconsciousness. The full formula looks like this: Perception=Conscious (Awareness x View) + Unconscious (Blindspots [Prejudices, Prejudgments, Imitation] Unexamined). Breaking this formula down will help make it comprehensible.

Awareness: Perception begins with your view of yourself and impacts what you see in your surroundings and others and, in turn, how they see you. Awareness comes through responding to events in your life and from self-discovery.

View: World view is the result of your previous experiences and acts as a series of filters which determine how you see your surroundings and others.

Blindspots: Attitudes and judgments that affect you but that you cannot see. These include:

Prejudices: Preconceived notions not based in fact

Pre-judgments: Opinions made before experiencing or interacting

Imitation: Attitudes and opinions based on someone else's perspective that are not examined; these may come from parents.

Unexamined: Blindspots that are not reconsidered or are taboo to reconsider; often cultural—religious, national or social.

We present our brands and ourselves from our perception point using the elements of personal branding. It is mirrored through your voice, body language, word choice and energy you project.

Although it is difficult to separate all these factors, the results are evident in people you meet.

Appendix III

Language

The way that you speak is a direct reflection of your brand, so a deeper understanding of what language is and what it does can help you better articulate your personal brand. This applies to your messaging and other ways in which you use words to promote your brand.

As stated in chapter seven, language is learned. This educational process begins at home and continues as the child enters school. As you learn to use language, you are subject to the people and elements around you. This is a significant part of your social conditioning.

SOCIAL CONDITIONING

Simultaneously interacting with others and our education form the linguistic arsenal built from social conditioning. This conditioning begins with the parent or guardian and continues with media, education and other social institutions such as community, government, clubs and organizations, judicial, law enforcement and economy/work.

Community is your neighborhood—a metropolis or town, a suburb or the inner city. It is a specific area where people reside and have a common government. Dialects can be created within these regions to the point where you recognize that someone is from a part of New York City or from Southern California. Your language is strongly influenced by your neighborhood. *Vernacular* refers to a dialect spoken by the ordinary people in a country or region. With the mobility of current culture, dialects can be obscured, but you often can detect one even if the person has moved around. You may not be able to distinguish the particular dialect as easily for those with multiple residences as for people who grow up and live in the same area for a majority of their lives. Dialects are easier to discern for those from other countries although some dialects are so distinctly from a region that you immediately recognize them. Where you live also influences your perception since what you experience is the basis for what you perceive, but the language of your locale has a further influence.

As with the Eskimos who have numerous words for snow, the physical and mental environment influence word choice, sentence structure and grammar. When speaking to her family, my wife's accent and language changes and has the Southern lilt. In addition, her shift in perception is evident since I spend a great deal of time around her. She speaks from a different perspective when talking with her mother or sisters, and this is also obvious to me when we go to family gatherings. I know when I am with my family, I have to make an effort to remain authentic and not fall into the role I had growing up. I listen to my language as a clue to how I am perceiving and interacting with them.

Community can also refer to a group with shared interests including professional organizations, spiritual assemblies and business alliances. The shared interest community usually grows out of a need or want, where a leader will emerge to form the organizational structure for it to thrive.

These organizations have their own argot or slang. In fact one of the best examples is the slang of teenagers. These words, phrases and phrasings are created to communicate only within the group until the words are used often enough to enter the general vocabulary. Professionals like doctors and lawyers have their own terminology and jargon.

Government creates its own language for official communications which you have to learn in order to deal with those organizations. Whether it be a form label or a statute on the books, you must learn this language to navigate through this social institution or enlist someone who "speaks the language" to help. Specialized vocabulary affects your view of the surroundings. There is a different feeling when walking into a government establishment; for most a certain formality is part of our perception.

You can find a club or organization for nearly anything you could imagine from horticulture to sailing. If you have not ever done so, go to the web and look at Meetup.com™ and you will be amazed at the variety. No matter how insignificant it may seem, each of the groups you belong to can and usually does influence your language. When I consider how I portray my personal brand as a writing coach and an author, I realize it differs from the way I present it to entrepreneurs as a publisher of business books. I recognize that I use a slightly altered vocabulary because I see individuals in these groups differently. There is much overlap but there is a distinct difference. My conversation is still within my brand but, as I like to say, "A good brand stretches."

If you have had any encounters with the justice system, you soon learn you need to be precise in your speech. Spending a lot of time in this arena will affect your language. With so many television shows containing elements of the legal system and law enforcement, you are bound to pick up vocabulary and attitudes. And the bottom line here is that the language and what it represents has impact on our perceptions.

Our economic environment builds crucial barriers and bridges to our financial health. How we think and speak about money is important, and most of the well-known books about financial success begin with one's attitude towards money. If you were raised and believe that money is the root of all evil, you will have a difficult time acquiring wealth. Much of the conversation you hear about money as you grow up sets your perception of prosperity. Most wealthy people agree that one's mindset about money is critical to success. This is one of the most apparent connections between language and perception.

WHAT MAKES UP OUR LANGUAGE?

Our language is comprised of six aspects:

- Vocabulary
- Syntax
- Semantics
- Poetic extensions
- Stories
- Dynamic range

Vocabulary is the words we know and use. The English language has over 1,000,000 words in dictionaries. The average speaker uses about 20,000 words and knows another 40,000. These numbers help us begin to understand more about word choice. It makes sense that the most common words can be used to convey a message to the largest audience. If you have a particular audience in mind, you may use specific words for them as indicated previously. Your word choice will determine who will understand and read your messages. How you will use those words is determined by your syntax.

Syntax

Syntax refers to word order. It is a set of rules about how words are placed in a sentence, and there may be a variety of ways those words can be arranged. We return to the concept of choice again, and your choices will be partially determined by what you perceive. Syntax also includes rules about punctuation. There is a great debate about whether syntax is learned or instinctual since we cannot detect how we first begin to speak. We may mimic vocabulary structures or may have an innate understanding of how to put sentences together. Whichever way we acquire syntax, we can adjust how we construct our sentences if we become more aware of our language.

Semantics

Semantics deals with the meaning of words. The prime distinction is the *denotative* meaning of a word and its *connotative* meaning.

The denotative meaning of a word is its standard definition as catalogued in dictionaries. This is a static meaning which we all basically understand. If we think of *dog*, we know it is a four-legged animal which has been domesticated as a pet and comes in a variety of breeds. However, if we say the word *dog* in passing, we have a general sense no matter what the breed. The denotative meaning is based on a shared consensus of what a word represents.

When I communicate *dog* to someone who has a cocker spaniel, he or she is probably going to picture a cocker spaniel. This is because that person is using the connotative meaning, one which is derived from the receiver's experience and/or by the surroundings. The connotative meaning is dependent on the listener.

Be as clear as possible in your messaging since your audience is most likely interpreting your words in a connotative sense.

Poetic Extensions (Creative Language)

These embellishments are used to paint pictures and do other magic with your words. Poetic extensions include analogies (metaphors and similes), idioms, allusions, alliteration, onomatopoeia, and rhyme.

Analogies are comparisons between unlike things. The two major forms are metaphor and simile. Examples of a metaphor are, "Her heart is broken" and "He is walking on air." Neither of these circumstances are literally true although it may feel that way. A metaphor allows us, through comparison, to attribute something from the second concept to the first which is not directly related. I am using a metaphor when I say, "I fly high when participants understand the power of their personal brands."

Like metaphors, similes also compare using the words *like* and *as.* You are familiar with ones that are cliché like "quick as a fox," "slow as molasses," or "cold as ice." Similes and metaphors work well when they are fresh and unexpected such as "noisy as a cricket" or "calm as a cadaver." A good metaphor or simile can stick in someone's mind for an extended period of time.

Idioms are embedded in our language. We don't recognize them most of the time, but they are phrases that do not make literal sense. These are so common we use them without thinking: "Take a walk," "speak your mind," "cross your fingers," "when pigs fly" and "tongue in cheek." We become aware of idioms when we learn a foreign language or when someone is learning English since our language is rich with idioms.

Alliteration and assonance are devices used frequently by advertisers. Alliteration is the repetition of an initial consonant sound such as *delightful dish* or *scintillating cymbals.* Note that the repetition is of the sound, not necessarily the consonant itself. Assonance is the repetition of a vowel sound. In the phrase, "I might want to fly" the underlined letters demonstrate assonance. These do not have to be the same letters. When I introduce my writing services I say, "Get that book out of your head and onto the web." The words *head* and *web* share the same vowel sound. They are near-rhymes but not actual rhymes.

Onomatopoeia

This strange sounding term refers to words that imitate the sound of what they are describing. Some examples are "buzzing bees," "rustling leaves," and "crash of dishes." Our words to describe animal sounds also use this device: "Moo," "quack," "meow" and "tweet." This is an effective device since it conjures up a picture through sound.

Rhyme

Finally consider rhyme. It is used in many jingles to help us remember products as well as in taglines. The use of rhyme is so widespread in what we hear every day that we take it for granted. However, its frequency in commercials and in daily life should prompt us to realize how it can help in promoting a personal brand.

Using a combination of these poetic devices can embolden your message. Spend some time thinking about what you are writing and speaking and your brand will progress.

Stories

We all know that one of the easiest ways to learn is hearing a story. Stories are part of our basic nature and are memorable long after statistics and facts are forgotten. Using a story to illustrate a point is the best way to make it indelible. The Bible, perhaps the most influential book, is a series of stories. We crave to see the latest movie or read the most recent book; our appetite for stories is unquenchable.

By telling a good story, you can use language to imprint your personal brand on others. Many of the best and most unforgettable television commercials are stories. The Budweiser ads with the Clydesdales and Dalmatian dogs are classic and stay with you for years. The 1984 black and white Apple commercial introducing the Macintosh was like a mini-movie, and, although you never learned the characters' names, you knew them and could identify with them.

Stories do not have to be fictional as the ones above. When you relate one of your own stories or those of other people, you can connect at that deep level with your audience. My personal story about how I became a writing coach and publisher enables my clients to share in what might also be their experiences.

One of my stories is about helping a friend publish a book that was not aligned with my publishing goals. The process was a struggle, and we could not meet eye to eye about editing, so there was tremendous conflict throughout our arrangement. In the end, we decided it was better for him to publish on his own, and I learned that not staying true to my brand was detrimental since it took so much energy to do the work and stay motivated. The book itself is good in its niche; it's just not a genre I want to publish. For authors and speakers, this is a cautionary tale about audience—find the right publisher or the organization that will appreciate your topic.

Fiction writers understand the power of story as do most non-fiction writers, and speakers use them throughout presentations. The draw to story goes back to early man.

Dynamic Range

How you speak your words can be more powerful than the words you use. One of the challenges in written communication is that the reader does not hear the inflections of voice. Perhaps this is the reason for the increased demand for audio books.

Whether you are a professional speaker or not, the way you use your voice for delivery of messages and daily communication has a mammoth effect on your brand. You can work on your voice if it is not optimal.

The deeper your voice is the more authority it commands. Think of the depth of the voices of national news anchors and many of the most admired speakers.

Once the concepts of language and perception are understood, you have the tools to deliver. The final step is to understand how to use these to promote the brand, yourself and your products and services. By promoting the brand and yourself effectively, others who you can serve will want your products and services.

Appendix IV

Impact

Who are the people you impact and how do you affect them? Some people have innate charisma and others seem to naturally follow them. Anyone can improve their influence once they understand what it is and how it operates. This appendix examines impact in more detail.

INFLUENCING STARTS WITH YOUR ATTITUDE TOWARDS YOURSELF

Negative thinkers rationalize why they should manipulate people to achieve their goals. From this perspective, they believe this is the only way they can get others to do what they want. This attitude has an impact on how they present themselves. It also reinforces the belief that they must continue to manipulate to be successful rather than trusting themselves and their products and services to provide value to their customers. Instead of providing benefits and value to influence, they feel pressure to exaggerate and/or misrepresent as tactics to convince.

People with strong faith in themselves and their brand build rapport quickly. They know themselves and that their words and actions will be aligned with the brand and deliver what is promised.

THREE WAYS YOU EXPERIENCE INFLUENCE

Influence can be experienced in three ways: self-experience, direct experience and indirect experience.

Self-experience

You have influence on others whether you are conscious of it or not. How you see yourself is conveyed in all your verbal and non-verbal communications. This impacts you and those with whom you communicate. Factors that influence negatively may come from a *lack of consciousness* reflected in bitterness, disgust, impatience, distrust and divisive thoughts and words. Factors that provide a beneficial influence are your positive thoughts and words, joys, passions, dreams and faith.

Direct Experience

This is real-time communication (in-person, telephone, teleconference and some online communications that are live). Direct experience is a dialogue between two or more persons. The groups with which you communicate this way include family, friends, coworkers, peers, acquaintances, employers and customers. These people are directly influenced by how you perceive yourself and how they view you. You are being influenced with the same principles.

This is the primary influence tool for speakers and authors who address groups.

Indirect Influence

This influence is with those who do not directly experience you. One example is when you send a resume to a company; they form an opinion before deciding whether to talk to you or not.

Television and forms of social media that are not interactive also have an indirect influence with a potentially high impact. Think of how well you think you know a celebrity although you have only watched them on TV. The rapport that video can create is impressive. Millions of dollars are spent on celebrity endorsements each year. Voters can be swayed and products sold by familiar figures on the screen.

Authors and bloggers influence indirectly as well through language, which has been covered. Using linguistic techniques, the writer intentionally or unintentionally has an impact on readers. Good writers know that the first few lines someone reads carry the most impact; authors who do not realize this will have a difficult time impressing a publisher or interesting a reader in what is to follow. One author I know rewrote his first chapter more than 10 times.

Other methods of this influence include your personal branding on websites, brochures, business cards, referrals, books, articles and audio recordings. Each of these helps you reach out and "touch" your potential clients and customers. Remember that it will take seven to 17 touches or more for others to recognize and get to know you and your brand.

WHAT FACTORS CREATE INFLUENCE

Credibility

How do you determine who and what you believe? The individuals you follow must present themselves and their offerings in a way that resonates with what is already familiar to you, or they need to provide compelling reasons and emotions to change your mind.

Let's look at the media to understand more about this characteristic. The most important quality of a news reporter is that he or she is reputable. The comforting images of Walter Cronkite, Mike Wallace and Huntley and Brinkley in the 1960s lent an air of knowledge and wisdom to the audience.[6]

When it was revealed that Dan Rather reported a story about a fake George Bush memo, forty years of credible reporting was suddenly forgotten. People ignored the fact that he had broken stories that were considered masterpieces of journalism, including the resignation of Richard Nixon and the Abu Ghraib scandal among others. But one big slip, the fake George Bush memo, and he was no longer seen as an authority.

So, what can you do to be credible? If you promise what you can deliver and deliver what you promise, your audience will believe you. At some time or another, however, you may slip up. If you have had a good track record, you should be able to recover. Most of your followers will be forgiving unless you frequently under-deliver or miss deadlines.

I was once told to put goodwill in the bank for clients so when a rainy day comes they will allow a misstep. Goodwill might include over-delivery or beating deadlines, doing something extra you never promised or throwing in a surprise bonus or discount. These activities are not done with the intention of getting something back but purely to delight your audience or clients.

Stay vigilant about your credibility and, if you encounter a challenge, do not ignore it; deal with it.

Messaging

What quotes do you remember? Whose speeches have influenced your life? Think of what was said and how it was related. Some of the most powerful messages such as in the "I Have a Dream" speech echo for decades.

If you are intentional about your messaging—spoken word, brochures, web copy and social media—your impact will increase.

Be consistent in what you present by adhering to your brand. Using your brand as a guiding factor can create uniformity, and people will recognize your communications even before they know the messages are from you.

Writing compelling copy takes time, but it is worth it. The right combination of reason and emotion is most powerful. Look for examples in television advertisements, signs around you, snippets you hear from others and in what you read. A well-turned phrase can remain in the mind of the reader or listener longer than you might expect. Create a memorable message and it will be the cornerstone of how people are influenced by your brand.

Presence

The importance of *being in the present* cannot be underestimated. Face-to-face interactions carry emotional and intuitive components that kick in before the first word is spoken. You get an impression of your communication partner as he or she does of you. In person, you are able to perceive smiles, body language and other gestures as described previously. As the conversation or interaction proceeds, the connection grows deeper.

The impact of your presence can be strengthened each time you meet someone new or see acquaintances and friends. Be aware of how you show up.

Relevance

If you share relevant information and knowledge that has value for your audience/clients/readers, they will appreciate it and be more open to your influence. Addressing their needs, desires and their dreams provides relevance. One method to achieve this is to listen.

Do you have the same elevator pitch for everyone? There is a better way. Instead of rattling off your same "speech," what if you asked a question about the other person to see what you could say that would be relevant to him or her? By asking first, you can customize your message *if* you think you can provide value. If you cannot help them, you may just want to tell them what you do. Even if you hand them a business card, they will remember you if what you say is relevant or forget you if you cannot add value to their lives.

Staying aware of your presence will help you have greater impact. Show up every day with your brand in mind and act from your I AM Statement to broadcast your personal brand.

Appendix V

Challenges to Your Personal Brand

The culture at large supports individuality in the name of competitive advantage. If you can use your differentiation to show how you are better than others in your field or endeavor, those around you are more than willing to cheer you on. Because competitive attitudes are deeply ingrained, and we are encouraged to enjoy boasting about our status or our newest possession, working to build a personal brand can be an uphill battle against learned competitive attitudes. Since this competition is reinforced in sports and business, it can be difficult for you to perceive a personal brand as valuable unless it is leveraged. This is where difficulties emerge both in defining that brand and implementing it for good.

These attitudes of competition prevent you from using your uniqueness to find and follow what can bring joy and simultaneously feed your soul and your body. With this pathway blocked by social barriers, most people find a way to fit in and do whatever will provide them with their necessities and desires. The number of people who are dissatisfied with their work increases daily, and, with the advent of new artificial intelligence, many are shuddering because they may be replaced tomorrow by a machine. This creates a sense of scarcity about work that then increases the perception of competition and the need to keep a firm grasp on what you now have. You may feel that you are doomed to *fit in* or give up your security.

Your training—from learning to stand in line in kindergarten to not rocking the boat in the workplace—is designed to shape you into a consumer and conformist. You learn what is acceptable and advisable to advance in your job. Have you ever had your hand slapped for doing a task in a new way? Have you heard these messages: *That's not the way it's supposed to be; we don't do it like that here.* After a few failures, most of us get the message and stop trying to follow our uniqueness until something *critical* happens. Then, you may feel it's too late to change.

What are some of the constraints you encounter daily? There are too many to delineate but most fall into one of these categories:

- Restrictions to impress acceptable behavior: As you grew up, you heard such maxims as "Speak only when you're spoken to," "Do not talk with your mouth full," and "Do what I say, not what I do."

- Role rules you learn in regard to gender and relationships (student/mentor, boss/employee, and husband/wife)

- Peer pressure: the urge to fit in which exploits you and drives you to act against your better instincts

- Acceptance based on fitting in: if you don't object to others' behavior, they will not object to yours. These are the concepts that prompted the poem *Mask*, which was shared in chapter six.

- Expectations of obedience: As children, you were expected to obey parents; as teens you obey the crowd; as workers you obey the boss.

Public pressure to conform encourages and rewards people for socially fitting in instead of allowing individuals to be themselves. This issue is rampant in our world.

What about you? If your need to fit in is greater than your desire for full participation in self-expression, aren't you hiding behind a mask? Are you the expression of your true self, or are you showing up in the world wearing a mask?

Even though this blind following is destructive to your true self, your mission and purpose, most will not or cannot resist. You give up your birthright to earn the money you think you need and acquire all the things that everyone around you has. I, for one, can look around my environment and see possessions I thought I needed that I don't use. I wonder why I purchased these things and cannot remember or don't realize it was because someone I knew had one and I felt I had to have it too. More than a few of you will be able to relate to this. What is worse is that you relinquish who you are for the almighty dollar. Money is not the root of all evil; chasing it indiscriminately well may be.

By following these patterns, you may create an identity crisis for yourself that will surface either in the present or in the future. When you give up who you are, you can conform and be happy for a while, but at some point, it is not enough. You may try to fill that void with more stuff until you see how pointless it is to use external things to try to fix what is internal.

Your mind is trained to look at the world through the filters (artificial lenses) it has created to fit in or to rebel. Your personality or ego views itself as a separate, limited unit. If you can drop this veil of personality, the benefits are limitless. Once you remove this mask, you are able to live a fuller and more meaningful life through your real self and your spirit, which can naturally inspire you.

In my many roles as a teacher, trainer, marketing consultant and coach, I have observed how vicious the hold social conditioning is on so many talented and gifted people. I've heard extremely bright individuals from a variety of backgrounds share the deep and agonizing pain they have suffered. I also have seen how many of them slipped in and out of uncertainty going through the *Purpose Powered Process* to reveal their genuine talents. One day they would show excitement for who they were; the next day they'd fall back into the comfortable routine of conformity. They fretted about being afraid to identify who they were really meant to become. I have had clients and those in workshops reschedule appointments (one-on-one) or follow-up conversations out of avoidance and express their frustrations through sadness. Others turned discussions into comedy routines to avoid talking about themselves, and still others blamed themselves for being "spineless." Because I've been through every one of these emotions myself and could identify, I was able to keep them moving forward in the personal branding process. I assured them that what they were feeling was normal and was a natural part of the process. They were on arduous journeys, removing the veils of their personalities that were shaped and conditioned since infancy, and they needed to be patient with themselves since that can be challenging at times.

Breaking away from social conditioning can be painful. Many live surface lives, wasting their most precious energies and talents by running as fast as they can to keep up with someone else's vision. Slowing down is frightening because they cannot fathom what would replace chasing previous goals and fear the emptiness they think would ensue. They are hungry for something more; yet, they find it too unpredictable and uncertain to make changes. Their lifestyles have trapped them. Getting real with their true selves might mean losing everything that has previously felt like security.

I recognize that society has taught you to sublimate your individual identity so that you can conform and blend in with everyone else. When making choice after choice—even small ones—that go against your authentic nature, it becomes easy to lose yourself altogether. How easy it is to forget what is meaningful and become confused. Instead of breaking out into a new style or livelihood that's authentically you, it is easier just to convince yourself that you have to follow the rules in order to earn a living, be accepted, fit in, get ahead, compete and prosper. Talk about not making sense! The only sense in this way of living is that it is non-sense. Deep down, many people are walking around in a state of self-loathing and that's a shame.

Those of you who have chosen the path of individuality and opted not to fit in may be challenged. More than likely, you've had to consistently fight against being snubbed by a society that would rather not deal with you. You may even question your sanity and think about conceding and giving in to external pressure. Others of you may be stuck in the fight against fitting in and seem to solve it by becoming a rebel. The rebel is the other end of the spectrum of the veiled personality. The way out of this quandary is to be deeply rooted in your passion, purpose and clarity.

Regardless of which end of the spectrum you cling to, rebel or socially-conditioned, the real question rests in how willing you are to fully embrace your uniqueness. How willing are you to naturally stand out without a need to fit in, compare or compete, or conversely rebel against the system? To do so is a matter of deciding to transcend the masked personality and discover how to make your uniqueness count in the world. You can reclaim your sense of reality by living in your personal brand. You can have authentic joy in your life!

Appendix VI
Exceptions - Difficult Clients

In order to be transparent, I want to let you know about our failures as well as successes mentioned throughout the book. Since beginning the workshops, I have had three participants who were unable to complete it.

The first was a young woman who had lost the joy in her life after being fired from her job. She was not in a relationship, and, once her job was gone, she no longer had the one thing she clutched to for her identity. Thinking it might help, I offered her the opportunity to attend for free since she also was having financial difficulties. Unfortunately, after the first hour, she left. Because she was so unhappy about her current circumstances, watching others find joy in the class made her feel worse than when she arrived. She was unwilling to change at the time, due in part to her negative perspective of her life. I am happy to relate that at a later time she did find another job and the relationship she craved.

The second was a gentleman who was unwilling to participate in the self-examination necessary due to religious views. I refunded his money no questions asked. He believed that his path was set out for him and, although he was not happy with what he was doing, he felt he had no choice. He was resigned to his perspective even though he was not satisfied. He decided to continue on the same path rather than pursue the self-examination process.

The third was the most challenging for me to understand. This fellow refused to participate in an exercise in which he chronicled his accomplishments. He had completed three-quarters of the process but declined to do this exercise. He had struggled earlier but with help had completed the other tasks. However, when it came to participation in a self-promotion exercise, he was either unwilling or unable. The irony was that he often boasted about his accomplishments and would often inflate their importance in daily conversation. Some deeper issue must have been at work.

Appendix VII
Footnotes and Files

FOOTNOTES

1 *http://www.nielsen.com/us/en/press-room/2013/global-consumers-more-likely-to-buy-new-products-from-familiar-b0.html*

2 *Reinventing Work: The Brand You 50,* Tom Peters, Publisher, 1999 p. 4

3 answers.google.com/answers/threadview?id=516517

4 *The Structure of the Psyche* (1927) in *Collected Works Vol. 8, The Structure and Dynamics of the Psyche,* p. 342

5 https://www.nngroup.com/articles/how-long-do-users-stay-on-web-pages/

6 https://en.wikipedia.org/wiki/List_of_news_presenters#American_news_anchors

FILES

These are the worksheets I have mentioned in the book:

Exercise 1   Uncovering Young Passions

Exercise 2   Uncovering Adult Passions

Exercise 3   Collate Your Lists

Exercise 4   Write Out Your Bucket List

Exercise 5   Examine Values

Exercise 6   Inner Purpose

Exercise 7   Your External Roles

Exercise 8   Who Are You Meant to Serve

Exercise 9   Depth Matrix

Exercise 10   Finding Your Distinctiveness

Exercise 11   Your Essential DNA Code

Exercise 12   The Archetypes

Exercise 13   I Am Questionnaire

Exercise 14   The I AM/Destiny Statement

Exercise 15   Tagline

Exercise 16   Brand Personality

Exercise 17   Integrating Your Results into Life

You can get pdf copies of these sent to you by registering with **Drew@ RealizationPress.com**. *You will be added to my list and can unsubscribe at any time.*

Acknowledgments

I wish to thank Genece Hamby, founder of Your Essential DNA, for beginning the program and Kristen Joy Laidig and Natalie Marie Collins for their help in finishing my writing.

I lovingly acknowledge my family, which created the foundation for my personal brand: Norman and Maxine Becker, Laura Becker, Pam Orren, Dinah Chetrit, and my ever-patient, wife Diana Henderson.

I enjoyed conversations with the gang at Night Kitchen: Remy Heskett, Steve Barsky, Paul Apollonia, Kevin Flanagan, Don Downs, and Brook Swindler.

Thanks to the staff at other cafes where I was welcomed: The Wake Zone and Common Grounds, both in Apex N.C.

Supportive Colleagues and Friends

All the following people have been supportive and given excellent advice: Martin Brossman, Whitney Hill, Frank Timberlake, Bill Davis, Divya Parekh, Omar McCallop, Robin Jennings, Alex Chango, Bob Crowley, Brent Garner, Gary Tomlinson, Bud Coggins, Cole Russing, Henry Miller, Janis Pettit, Katie Gailes, Lori King, Michael Garr, Michelle Hill, Misty Campbell, Pat Howlett, Dee and David Shell, Gayle Allen, Scott Anspach and Alexius Benedict at *Active Bodez*, Theresa LK. Bassett, Alice Fuller, Michelle Hill, Eddie Morgan, Denise Dominguez, Dianne Daniels, Rick Barnes, Sarah Littlejohn, Annie Flood, Heather Nethery and Margo Arrowsmith. I would also like to thank those who may have slipped my mind but should be included.

Faithful Beta Readers

These people helped with suggestions to make the book more readable: Valorie McNabb Pope, Robin Jennings, Bobby Mehdwan, Marie Raymond, Ladey Adey and Gia Brainerd.

Other Architects

Other Your Essential DNA architects who added to the process include: Elisabeth Gorthschacher, Jody Nichols, Dana Cilmi, Ruth Ledesma, Evelyn McCauley, Bobbie Kimball, and Peter Metzner.

Purpose Powered Process Graduates

I also learned each time I taught the workshops and want to thank these graduates: Marsha Burger, Dianne Evans, Michael Stein, Sally Curry, Ayse Durmaz, Asha Gleason, Sandra Polinco, Cyndy Ratfcliffe, Marge Randol, Michelle Moss, Jane Norton, Vicky Olive, Bonnie Livengood, Stephanie McDilda, Nancy Long, Marty Lynch, Maggie McGlynn, Ya Mei Mandeville, Viki Ichikawa, Michael Sarni, Marcia Adelberg, Judy Hamberg, Derek Campbell, Livleen Kahlon, Carly Mason, Lourdes Mendez, Carolyn Anderson, Elizabeth Jones, John Wyatt, Rose Degen, Mary Fulton, Barbara Carr Brossman, Tim Palo, Jane Ivey, Susan Cole, Vickie Bevnour, Theresa Carter, Aaron Mangal, Sarah Rowland, Jean Young, Ron Young, Neesa Moloney, Beth Savino, Arleen Hannich, Rosemary Martin, Kimberly Mears, Michele Wittman, Edie Raether, Leslie Scott, Chelle Kingman, Galin Panchev, Geoff Hawkins, Elke Brand, Michael Grohs, Shawn Leehans, Kristi Drum, Kathie McCutcheon, Bruce King, Jen Conaway, Karen Free, Amy Sky, Angela Lin, Josh Howard, Diana Howard, Renee Porter, Gloria Andrioli, Sylethia Davis and Marirose K. Steigerwald.

Networking Buddies

Thanks to the folks with whom I discussed personal branding at the Apex Small Business Network, the the Fuquay-Varina Small Business Network and elsewhere: Jessica Yee of *Impact Stationery and Gifts,* Bob Bedi of *Media Integrations,* Suzanne Yaeger of *Your Smart Office,* Jessica Bolton of *Magnolia and Vine,* Christa Davidson, Frieda Lin, Nancy Ruffner of *Navigate NC,* Sean Obrien, Richard Bobholz of *Law++,* Mark Esposito of *Connectmatic,* Tim McCauley of *Get Visual Business Solutions,* Pat Fontana of *Words Working,* Janet Bowen of *Moe's Southwest Grill,* Marlana Semenza of *Marlana Semenza Photography,* Angie Ceroli of *2 Cups Green Tea,* Shannon Flaherty and Barbara Belicic of *the Apex Chamber of Commerce,* Katrina Fraley of *The Original Relocation Guide,* Paul Hanlon of *Apex Health Insurance,* Darlene Hawley of *Mane Design,* Brian Frost of *Guardian Home Technologies,* Joe Novara, Debra Mathias of *Connect to Clients,* Amy Osborne, Denise Gibbon of *Above the Dotted Line,* Jigna Shah CPA, Melanie Hampton of *Serenity Pet Massage,* Greg Harris of *Leapfrog Lawncare,* Judy Julian of *Go4LessNow Travel,* Troy Krischner of *Space Krafters,* Andy Kraft of *Spectrum,* Dorena Kohrs of *Breathing Room Professional Organizers,* Paul Kreader of *Northside Realty,* Janet Mason of *Horse and Buddy,* Bill Laundon of *Edward Jones,* Chantal LeBlanc of *Real Property Management,* Nancy MacCreery of *Broad Reach Marketing Services,*

Frank Manson, *Principal Financial Group*, Tina Owen of *Damsel in Defense*, Kelli Peele of *First Citizens Bank*, Christa Phillips of *Arbonne*, Kara Ramsey of *EyeCare for You*, Megan Reed of *Peak Wellness and Chiropractic*, JV Miller of *Broadmoar Consulting Group*, Teresa Robinson of *Reaching Higher*, Mindy Schrager of *Systems of Change*, Kathy Simmers of *Melaleuka*, Dori Staehle of *Rock the Next Stage*, Melissa Van of *AABS*, Jim Vogel from *IMU Social Media*, David Newton of *SEO Specialist*, and James Wong and Virginia Johnson of *Empowered Ideas/Fuquay Coworking*.

Other Books by the Author

POETRY

I Fell for 13 Dreamers

Writers Block Series

Book 1

Interviewing Quick Guide: The Art and the Craft
    Available at http://amzn.to/1CVo4KS

Book 2

Write a Non-Fiction Book in 4 Weeks
    Available at http://amzn.to/1CVo4KS

Book 3

Write a Fiction Book in 4 Weeks
    Available at http://amzn.to/1CVo4KS